Lead with AI

Lead with AI is your roadmap to thriving in a world where artificial intelligence reshapes every aspect of business and leadership. This book gives you the vision, tools, and confidence to harness AI, inspire your team, and stay ahead of disruption.

Written by

ERIC LEBOUTHILLIER

AcraSolution | 2025 1st Edition
www.acrasolution.com

Preface

Who this book is for

- **Business leaders, managers, and executives** who want to understand how AI is transforming organizations and how to adapt their leadership style.

- **Entrepreneurs and innovators** seeking practical ways to leverage AI to grow, scale, and future-proof their businesses.

- **Professionals and students** preparing for the future of work and aiming to become valuable leaders in the AI-driven economy.

- **Organizations** looking to build AI-ready teams and cultures of innovation.

What to expect from this book

- A **clear explanation** of how AI is reshaping industries and the future of business.
- **Leadership strategies** for managing people, projects, and organizations in the age of intelligent machines.
- **Practical tools and frameworks** to apply AI in decision-making, productivity, and innovation.
- **Case studies** from global companies already succeeding with AI adoption.
- Guidance on **building AI-ready teams** and overcoming resistance to digital transformation.
- A dedicated chapter on **ethics, trust, and responsible leadership** with AI.
- A **step-by-step roadmap** to becoming an AI leader—starting today and scaling into the future.

☑ By the end of the book, readers won't just *understand* AI—they'll know how to **lead with it**, drive innovation, and thrive in the digital era.

Copyright © 2025
All Rights Reserved

LEGAL DISCLAIMER

This publication is intended solely for informational and educational purposes. It does not constitute legal, financial, medical, or professional advice. The content is not a substitute for consultation with qualified experts or licensed professionals in the relevant fields.

Portions of this work have been created or assisted by artificial intelligence (AI) tools. While every reasonable effort has been made to review, fact-check, and edit the content for clarity and accuracy, AI-generated information may occasionally contain errors, omissions, or generalized statements. The author and publisher do not guarantee the accuracy, completeness, or reliability of the information provided.

Readers are strongly encouraged to seek independent advice tailored to their personal circumstances from qualified legal, financial, healthcare, or compliance professionals before making decisions or taking action based on this content.

References to specific products, services, companies, websites, or technologies do not imply endorsement or affiliation unless explicitly stated. All trademarks and brand names mentioned remain the property of their respective owners.

The author and publisher disclaim any liability, loss, or risk incurred directly or indirectly from the use or misuse of this publication. This includes, but is not limited to, damages of any kind — including incidental, special, or consequential — arising out of the reliance on the material presented.

All references to laws, regulations, security standards, or industry guidelines are intended for general awareness only and may not reflect the most current legal developments. This publication is not intended to create, and receipt does not constitute, a client relationship with the author, publisher, or any affiliated entity.

By reading, accessing, or applying the content in this publication, you agree to do so at your own risk. If you do not accept these terms, you are advised to discontinue use of this material immediately.

Table of Contents

CHAPTER 1

The Call to Lead with AI

Why Leadership Is Being Redefined in the AI Era

Artificial intelligence is not just another technology—it is a force that is reshaping the foundations of business, society, and human potential. Just as the industrial revolution demanded a new kind of leader who could manage machines and large-scale production, the AI era requires leaders who can navigate complexity, uncertainty, and speed at levels humanity has never experienced before. Leadership is being redefined because the tools, the pace, and the stakes have changed.

From Information Scarcity to Information Abundance

For most of history, leaders held power because they had access to knowledge others did not. Decision-making was guided by experience, intuition, and the selective information available at the time. Today, AI systems process millions of data points in seconds, surfacing insights no human could reasonably generate. The leader's role is no longer to be the sole authority of knowledge but to ask the right questions, interpret AI-driven insights, and turn them into actionable strategies.

This transition is profound: leadership shifts from *knowing* to *sense-making*. The leader is not the smartest person in the room but the one who can best integrate human judgment with machine intelligence.

The Acceleration of Change

The half-life of skills is shrinking. A technical skill that was relevant five years ago may already be obsolete today. AI accelerates this cycle, making adaptation—not mastery of one static domain—the defining trait of successful leadership. For example, leaders at companies like Netflix or Tesla are not celebrated for sticking to rigid playbooks but for continuously reinventing themselves and their organizations in response to new AI-driven opportunities.

This requires a new leadership muscle: *adaptive foresight*. Leaders must anticipate not just how AI affects their industry today but how it may reshape customer expectations, competitive dynamics, and workforce needs tomorrow.

The Human Dimension of AI

Ironically, the rise of intelligent machines elevates the importance of distinctly human skills. As AI takes over tasks that are repetitive, analytical, or predictive, the differentiating factor for leaders becomes emotional intelligence, vision, and ethical judgment. Employees and stakeholders will increasingly look to leaders not for technical instructions but for meaning, trust, and alignment.

Consider healthcare: AI can now detect diseases with remarkable accuracy, but patients still rely on doctors and hospital leaders to communicate care, build trust, and make ethical decisions. In the AI era, leaders are not competing with machines—they are amplifying human value in partnership with machines.

Leading Beyond the Organization

In the past, leadership influence was largely contained within the boundaries of an organization. In the AI era, decisions made by one company can ripple across industries and societies. A single algorithm used in hiring or lending, for instance, can shape economic opportunities for thousands of people. Leaders are no longer just responsible for shareholder value—they carry responsibility for the broader impact of AI on communities, equity, and trust.

This expands the definition of leadership from *operational management* to *societal stewardship*. The AI leader must think beyond quarterly earnings and recognize the long-term implications of their choices.

A Redefinition of Authority

The authority of leaders used to be tied to hierarchy and control. In an AI-driven world, authority comes from credibility, transparency, and the ability to collaborate across disciplines. Teams expect leaders who are willing to learn alongside them, experiment with new technologies, and admit uncertainty when navigating uncharted territory.

The companies winning in the AI age are led by individuals who embrace humility and curiosity over rigid command-and-control. Authority is redefined not as the power to dictate but as the ability to orchestrate collaboration between humans and machines.

The Takeaway

Leadership is being redefined in the AI era because the nature of knowledge, change, responsibility, and authority has fundamentally shifted. No leader can rely on traditional playbooks of experience and hierarchy alone. To thrive, leaders must blend the precision of AI with the vision, adaptability, and ethics that only humans can provide. Growth in this new era comes from embracing this dual role: leveraging intelligent machines while elevating what makes us most human.

The Difference Between AI Managers vs. AI Leaders

The arrival of artificial intelligence has drawn a new line between those who *manage* technology and those who *lead* with it. While both roles are essential, they operate on fundamentally different levels of influence and vision. An AI manager ensures the machine runs; an AI leader ensures the machine transforms. Understanding this distinction is critical for anyone who aspires to shape the future rather than simply maintain the present.

Managers Focus on Tools, Leaders Focus on Purpose

An AI manager sees AI primarily as a tool to optimize existing processes. They ask: *How can this software reduce costs? How can it improve efficiency?* Their horizon is tactical. For example, a retail operations manager might deploy AI chatbots to handle customer inquiries, cutting call center wait times. It's effective, measurable, and practical—but it doesn't fundamentally change the way the organization creates value.

An AI leader, on the other hand, frames the same technology within a larger vision: *How can AI help us reimagine the customer experience? How could it create new business models or open up entirely new markets?* Instead of limiting AI to automation, they see it as an engine of transformation. Jeff Bezos, for example, didn't just use AI to recommend books; he used it to redefine global commerce through personalization, logistics, and cloud infrastructure.

Managers Optimize, Leaders Reinvent

AI managers thrive in optimization. They refine, streamline, and measure. Their role is crucial for stability and scalability, but it is inherently conservative—they protect the present.

AI leaders thrive in reinvention. They ask questions that challenge the status quo: *If AI can forecast demand more accurately, should our supply chain model remain the same at all? If AI can generate new designs, what does that mean for our product development cycle?* They use AI not just to improve the current system but to build systems that were previously unimaginable.

Consider the difference between a bank manager who uses AI to detect fraud faster versus a fintech leader who uses AI to design entirely new financial products for underbanked populations. Both add value, but only one expands the boundaries of what the industry can be.

Managers Control, Leaders Empower

AI managers often focus on control: dashboards, KPIs, compliance, and performance metrics. This is necessary but limited. If overemphasized, it risks turning AI into a surveillance tool that breeds fear and resistance among employees.

AI leaders, in contrast, use AI to empower people. They recognize that while machines may handle data, creativity and empathy remain human strengths. Leaders design AI systems that free employees from repetitive tasks so they can focus on higher-value work. For example, in healthcare, some hospitals use AI to automate administrative work, giving doctors more time to connect with patients. The difference lies in intent: is AI about controlling workers, or about unleashing their potential?

Managers Follow, Leaders Shape

The AI manager typically implements what the market already validates. They adopt proven tools when competitors have shown their effectiveness. Their risk appetite is low because their role is to minimize disruption.

The AI leader, by contrast, shapes the market itself. They adopt early, experiment boldly, and influence not just company strategy but industry direction. Think of Satya Nadella at Microsoft: rather than waiting for consensus, he bet early and heavily on AI integration across the company's product suite, positioning Microsoft as a leader in enterprise AI. That is the hallmark of leadership—acting before certainty.

The Takeaway

The difference between AI managers and AI leaders is the difference between maintenance and transformation. Managers keep the system efficient; leaders redefine what the system can achieve. In the AI era, organizations need both—but only leaders will create the breakthroughs that move industries forward. Growth, therefore, depends not on how well we manage AI, but on how courageously we lead with it.

Shifting from Fear of Disruption to Future Opportunity

Every technological revolution brings uncertainty, but few have sparked as much anxiety as artificial intelligence. The narrative often begins with headlines about job loss, automation, or machines replacing humans. This fear, though understandable, limits vision. Leaders who fixate on disruption see only threats; leaders who reframe disruption as opportunity see possibilities others overlook. The difference between the two mindsets can determine whether an organization stagnates or thrives.

The Cost of Fear-Based Leadership

Fear is not a sustainable strategy. Leaders who respond defensively to AI often delay adoption, waiting for others to test and validate technologies first. By the time they move, competitors have already gained the advantage. This happened in retail when companies like Blockbuster dismissed digital transformation while Netflix reimagined entertainment through algorithms and personalization. The result wasn't just disruption—it was extinction.

Fear-based leadership also paralyzes teams. When employees sense uncertainty or dread from the top, innovation shuts down. Instead of asking, *"How can AI make us better?"* people ask, *"When will AI replace me?"* A culture of fear stifles curiosity—the very quality AI leaders need most.

Opportunity-Oriented Thinking

Leaders who view AI as a catalyst for growth shift the conversation from loss to leverage. They ask: *What new value can we create with these tools? What problems that once seemed impossible can we now solve?* Opportunity-oriented thinking reframes AI as an ally.

Take logistics: while some worry about autonomous trucks replacing drivers, visionary companies explore how AI can reduce accidents, lower costs, and create entirely new roles in fleet management, predictive maintenance, and AI operations oversight. Instead of focusing only on jobs that may disappear, they invest in jobs that will emerge.

The Psychology of Reframing

Cognitive psychology shows that humans are wired to focus more on threats than opportunities—a phenomenon known as *negativity bias*. AI amplifies this instinct because it challenges our sense of control. But leaders can actively reframe the narrative. By highlighting success stories, setting bold visions, and showing employees how AI can enhance rather than diminish their roles, leaders shift collective attention toward progress.

For example, when JPMorgan introduced AI to automate legal document reviews, it could have triggered fear among attorneys. Instead, leadership emphasized how lawyers would be freed from monotonous tasks to focus on higher-value strategic work. The result: AI adoption was embraced rather than resisted.

Practical Steps to Shift From Fear to Opportunity

1. **Communicate transparently** – Explain not just what AI is being introduced, but *why*. Uncertainty breeds fear; clarity breeds trust.
2. **Highlight human-AI complementarity** – Show explicitly how AI augments human strengths rather than replaces them.
3. **Celebrate quick wins** – Share examples where AI saved time, improved customer experience, or opened new opportunities. Momentum builds confidence.
4. **Invest in reskilling** – Replace fear with growth by providing pathways for employees to adapt and thrive.

Fear vs. Opportunity at Scale

On a larger scale, the same mindset shapes industries and nations. Countries that see AI primarily as a threat may focus heavily on regulation and protectionism, slowing innovation. Those that see AI as an opportunity—investing in talent, infrastructure, and entrepreneurship—position themselves as leaders of the next economic wave.

The Takeaway

Shifting from fear of disruption to future opportunity is not naïve optimism; it is strategic leadership. Fear locks leaders into defensive postures, while opportunity unlocks vision, innovation, and growth. The organizations that will thrive in the AI era are those led by individuals who resist paralysis, embrace uncertainty, and turn disruption into a springboard for progress.

The New Responsibilities of Digital-Era Leaders

Artificial intelligence has not only changed how organizations operate—it has expanded what leaders are accountable for. In the digital era, leadership is no longer just about financial performance, operational efficiency, or shareholder returns. It is about guiding organizations through technological transformation while protecting trust, enabling growth, and ensuring responsible use of powerful tools. The weight of responsibility has grown heavier, but so has the opportunity to make lasting impact.

From Decision-Making to Sense-Making

In the past, leaders were expected to make decisions by relying on expertise, intuition, and limited data. Today, AI generates more information than any leader could process alone. The role has shifted from *making every decision* to *making sense of decisions AI recommends*. This requires new skills: critical questioning of algorithms, understanding data limitations, and ensuring that human judgment remains at the center.

For example, an AI model may recommend which customers are most likely to churn. A manager might take the output at face value. A leader, however, digs deeper: *What data was the model trained on? Could it be biased? Are there human factors the AI cannot capture?* Leadership in the digital era means ensuring AI informs decisions without replacing discernment.

Ethical Stewardship

With great technological power comes heightened ethical responsibility. AI can unintentionally reinforce biases, threaten privacy, or be misused for short-term gain. Digital-era leaders are responsible for ensuring that their organizations do not chase efficiency at the expense of fairness, transparency, or trust.

This responsibility is not theoretical. Consider recruiting: AI-driven hiring tools have been found to favor candidates of certain demographics, excluding equally qualified individuals. Leaders cannot outsource fairness to machines—they must set ethical standards, demand transparency, and ensure systems align with company values and societal expectations.

Empowering Human Potential

Another responsibility of modern leaders is to ensure technology amplifies human talent rather than diminishes it. As automation grows, so does the fear of irrelevance among employees. Leaders must actively counter this by showing how AI can free teams from low-value work and by investing in reskilling.

For instance, when Accenture began rolling out AI-driven automation across its global workforce, leadership launched massive upskilling programs to prepare employees for new roles in data science, AI operations, and digital consulting. The message was clear: technology may change jobs, but leadership ensures people are not left behind.

Building Trust in a Data-Driven World

Trust has always been central to leadership, but in the AI era, the stakes are higher. Customers, employees, and regulators are asking new questions: *How is my data being used? Who has access to it? What safeguards protect me?* Leaders cannot delegate these answers to IT teams—they must own them.

Failing to do so risks more than technical issues; it undermines reputation. Data breaches, algorithmic bias, or misuse of AI can erode customer loyalty overnight. Digital-era leaders carry the responsibility to ensure trust is not an afterthought but a foundational principle guiding strategy and operations.

Anticipating Societal Impact

Finally, leaders must broaden their perspective beyond organizational boundaries. AI adoption affects entire ecosystems—supply chains, industries, communities, and even democracy itself. Leaders are now called to think about the second- and third-order consequences of their choices. For example, introducing AI-driven gig platforms may increase efficiency but also reshape labor markets in ways that create precarity for workers. A responsible leader does not ignore these ripple effects but actively works to mitigate harm.

The Takeaway

The new responsibilities of digital-era leaders extend far beyond managing profits and processes. They include sense-making in a world of abundant data, ethical stewardship of powerful tools, empowerment of human potential, building trust through transparency, and anticipating societal impact. Leadership has always been about accountability—but in the AI era, the scope of accountability has expanded. Growth now depends on leaders who are not only technologically competent but also ethically grounded and human-centered.

Why the World Doesn't Just Need AI Specialists—It Needs AI Leaders

The rise of artificial intelligence has created enormous demand for technical talent—engineers, data scientists, and machine learning specialists. Their work is essential for building the systems that power industries. But technical expertise alone is not enough. Without leadership, AI risks becoming a collection of impressive tools without direction, alignment, or responsibility. The world needs leaders who can bridge the gap between technical possibility and human purpose.

Specialists Build, Leaders Guide

AI specialists are masters of algorithms, data pipelines, and model training. They can create systems that diagnose diseases, predict customer behavior, or automate workflows. But they are not necessarily tasked with deciding *why* a system should be built, *who* it serves, or *how* it aligns with long-term strategy.

That responsibility falls to AI leaders. They guide teams toward applications that create value, align with ethics, and support organizational goals. For example, a team of specialists might develop a cutting-edge image recognition model. A leader asks: *Should we use it for healthcare diagnostics, retail analytics, or surveillance? What risks come with each path?* The technology itself cannot answer these questions—leadership can.

The Risk of a Specialist-Only Mindset

When organizations rely solely on specialists, AI projects risk becoming siloed experiments without impact. Many companies have invested heavily in AI pilots only to find them stuck in "proof of concept" mode—technically impressive but commercially irrelevant. This happens when technical achievement is not paired with strategic leadership.

Consider the difference between developing a chatbot prototype and reimagining an entire customer service strategy powered by AI. The first requires specialists; the second requires leadership. Without leaders, AI risks being underutilized, misapplied, or even harmful.

Leaders Translate Complexity Into Vision

AI is inherently complex, often opaque even to the people building it. Leaders play a crucial role in translating that complexity into a vision that employees, investors, and customers can rally around. They make AI understandable and actionable.

For instance, when a CEO communicates how AI will improve both employee productivity and customer experience, they transform abstract algorithms into a story of progress. Specialists ensure the system works; leaders ensure people believe in its purpose.

Leaders Carry Ethical Accountability

Specialists may flag potential biases or risks in AI systems, but it is leaders who must decide what trade-offs are acceptable and what guardrails must be in place. The accountability for ethical use of AI lies with leadership. When a facial recognition tool misidentifies certain demographics, it is not just a technical flaw—it is a leadership failure if the issue is ignored.

This is why governments, regulators, and societies increasingly demand not only technical competence from organizations but also visible, responsible leadership. The question is not just *can* we build it, but *should* we?

Leaders Unlock Scale and Integration

Finally, while specialists can build powerful tools, only leaders can integrate those tools into the fabric of an organization. True transformation comes when AI is woven into strategy, culture, and customer experience. Leaders ensure AI adoption is not a one-off project but a sustained evolution.

Satya Nadella's leadership at Microsoft illustrates this well. While the company employs thousands of AI specialists, it was leadership that articulated a vision—AI to empower every person and organization on the planet. Specialists built the tools; leadership ensured those tools reshaped the business.

The Takeaway

The world needs AI specialists to build the systems of tomorrow, but it needs AI leaders even more to give those systems direction, purpose, and accountability. Specialists answer *how*. Leaders answer *why*. Growth in the AI era requires both—but without leaders, AI risks becoming powerful yet purposeless. The future will be shaped not just by the brilliance of those who code, but by the vision and responsibility of those who lead.

CHAPTER 2

The Future of AI in Business

AI as the Next General-Purpose Technology

Some technologies are incremental—they improve existing processes without fundamentally reshaping society. Others are *general-purpose technologies* (GPTs): innovations so transformative that they redefine economies, industries, and human life. Electricity, the steam engine, and the internet fall into this category. Artificial intelligence now stands alongside them. To understand AI as a general-purpose technology is to grasp not only its power but also its inevitability.

What Makes a Technology "General-Purpose"

Economists define a general-purpose technology by three criteria: it is pervasive, it improves over time, and it spawns complementary innovations across sectors. AI meets all three.

- **Pervasive**: AI can be applied across virtually every domain—healthcare, finance, manufacturing, education, and beyond.
- **Improving Over Time**: With more data, better algorithms, and cheaper computing, AI becomes more powerful the more it is used.
- **Catalyst for Innovation**: AI enables new applications that would be impossible without it, from drug discovery to autonomous vehicles.

This is why experts compare AI not to a single product but to electricity: it is not about *what AI does* in one instance, but *what it enables* everywhere.

Lessons from Past GPTs

History shows that general-purpose technologies reshape the world in phases. When electricity was first introduced, many factories simply replaced steam engines with electric motors. Productivity gains were modest until leaders redesigned factories entirely—creating assembly lines, new workflows, and new industries. Similarly, when the internet emerged, early applications mirrored old processes (online brochures, email as digital letters). Only later did leaders reimagine business models—e-commerce, social media, digital marketplaces.

AI is at a similar inflection point. Many organizations are still in the "substitution" phase—using AI to automate existing tasks. The real transformation will come when leaders rethink systems and business models from the ground up.

The Transformative Reach of AI

Already, AI's reach shows its general-purpose nature:

- **Healthcare**: AI assists in diagnosing diseases, predicting outbreaks, and personalizing treatments.
- **Finance**: Algorithms manage risk, detect fraud, and power algorithmic trading.
- **Manufacturing**: Predictive maintenance, quality control, and supply chain optimization are becoming AI-driven.
- **Education**: Personalized learning platforms adapt to individual students in real time.

And this is only the beginning. As AI systems advance, they will underpin entirely new industries, just as the internet gave rise to e-commerce and social media.

Why Leaders Must Recognize AI as a GPT

For leaders, the significance of AI as a general-purpose technology is twofold. First, it means AI is not optional. Just as no modern company can function without electricity or the internet, soon no competitive organization will function without AI. Second, it means the greatest opportunities are not in isolated applications but in systemic reimagination.

Leaders who treat AI as a peripheral add-on will fall behind. Leaders who embrace AI as foundational will create organizations that evolve with the technology, compounding their advantage over time.

The Takeaway

Artificial intelligence is not just another tool—it is a general-purpose technology, reshaping the foundations of the global economy. Like electricity and the internet, its true power lies not in isolated use cases but in the systemic transformation it enables. Growth in the AI era will come from leaders who recognize this inevitability early and act decisively to reimagine their organizations around it.

Major Industries Already Transformed by AI

Artificial intelligence is no longer a future promise—it is a present reality reshaping industries at scale. Some sectors are further along the curve than others, but the common pattern is clear: AI is not just improving efficiency; it is rewriting the rules of competition. Leaders who recognize these shifts gain the advantage of foresight, while those who ignore them risk obsolescence.

Healthcare: From Diagnosis to Discovery

In healthcare, AI has already moved from experimental to indispensable. Machine learning models now assist radiologists in detecting tumors earlier than human eyes alone. AI-driven drug discovery platforms dramatically shorten the timeline for identifying new treatments, as demonstrated during the COVID-19 pandemic when AI systems helped map potential vaccine candidates in record time.

Hospitals are also using AI for operational improvements— predicting patient admissions, optimizing staff schedules, and reducing wait times. The result is not only better care but also a more sustainable healthcare system.

Yet the true transformation lies ahead: AI promises to make medicine more personalized. Algorithms can analyze genetic data, lifestyle patterns, and health histories to tailor treatments to each individual. Leaders in healthcare must now navigate not just technical adoption but also ethical and regulatory challenges around patient data and trust.

Finance: Intelligence at Scale

The financial sector was one of the earliest adopters of AI, and today, algorithms touch nearly every aspect of banking and investment. Fraud detection systems use AI to spot anomalies in real time, saving billions in potential losses. Robo-advisors democratize wealth management by providing personalized investment strategies at scale. High-frequency trading firms rely on AI to process vast amounts of market data in milliseconds, gaining competitive edges that no human trader could match.

But the transformation is not only operational. AI is expanding access: micro-lending platforms use AI to assess creditworthiness in markets where traditional banking systems fail, opening financial inclusion to millions who were previously excluded. Leaders in finance face the challenge of balancing innovation with responsibility, ensuring transparency in systems that directly impact people's economic well-being.

Logistics and Supply Chains: Precision at Scale

The complexity of global supply chains makes them fertile ground for AI transformation. Companies like Amazon and UPS use predictive algorithms to optimize routes, reduce fuel costs, and improve delivery times. During the pandemic, AI models were critical in forecasting demand fluctuations and helping businesses adapt in real time.

Warehouses are becoming semi-autonomous ecosystems, where robots powered by AI handle inventory, while predictive systems forecast when and where products will be needed. These changes increase resilience, efficiency, and scalability. Leaders in logistics now see AI not as a cost-saving measure but as the backbone of supply chain agility.

Education: Learning Without Limits

AI is also beginning to transform education. Personalized learning platforms, such as those used in online education, adapt to individual student progress, ensuring that learners receive targeted support when they struggle and accelerated paths when they excel. AI-driven tutoring systems provide one-on-one support at scale, something traditional classrooms could never achieve.

Administrative tasks, from grading to enrollment management, are increasingly automated, allowing teachers to focus more on human connection and less on paperwork. Leaders in education face a unique responsibility: using AI to close gaps in access and equity rather than widen them.

The Takeaway

Healthcare, finance, logistics, and education already show how AI transforms industries not by automating tasks alone but by enabling entirely new ways of operating. These sectors demonstrate both the promise and the responsibility of AI. For leaders, the lesson is clear: transformation is no longer hypothetical. It is here, and the organizations that thrive will be those that embrace AI with vision, responsibility, and speed.

Where AI Is Creating New Billion-Dollar Opportunities

Artificial intelligence is not only transforming existing industries—it is creating entirely new markets and billion-dollar opportunities. Just as the internet birthed e-commerce, social media, and digital marketplaces, AI is unlocking frontiers that were once unimaginable. Leaders who spot these openings early position their organizations to ride the next wave of growth rather than chase it.

AI in Drug Discovery and Biotechnology

Traditional drug development takes over a decade and billions of dollars, with high rates of failure. AI is changing that equation. By analyzing vast datasets of molecular structures and biological interactions, AI models can identify promising compounds in months, not years. Startups and pharmaceutical giants alike are pouring resources into AI-driven biotech platforms. This is not a marginal improvement—it is the foundation of a trillion-dollar healthcare revolution.

The opportunity extends beyond big pharma. AI enables personalized medicine, where treatments are tailored to genetic profiles. Leaders who invest in this space are not only tapping into massive markets but also redefining the future of human longevity and wellness.

AI in Climate and Energy Solutions

Climate change is one of humanity's greatest challenges, and AI is emerging as a critical tool in the fight. AI models optimize energy grids, predict equipment failures in renewable plants, and design more efficient solar panels and batteries. Companies that leverage AI to accelerate the energy transition are positioning themselves in what could be the largest economic transformation of the 21st century.

Consider agriculture: AI-driven precision farming reduces water usage, predicts crop yields, and minimizes pesticide reliance. These solutions not only improve sustainability but also open multi-billion-dollar opportunities in global food security.

AI-Powered Creative Industries

Generative AI is redefining creativity. Tools that generate text, images, music, and video are giving rise to entirely new markets—AI-powered design, virtual entertainment, and personalized content at scale. This is more than a novelty. Imagine advertising agencies that generate hyper-targeted campaigns in minutes or film studios that create virtual actors and scenes without traditional production costs.

Some skeptics argue AI-generated creativity threatens human artists. The more accurate view is that it expands creative capacity, much like photography did not kill painting but gave rise to new art forms. Leaders in media, gaming, and design who embrace generative AI are already capturing billion-dollar valuations.

AI Agents and Autonomous Enterprises

One of the most disruptive opportunities lies in AI agents—autonomous systems that can perform complex tasks across software platforms without constant human input. Imagine an AI agent that manages procurement, negotiates with suppliers, or runs entire marketing campaigns end-to-end. This shift toward *autonomous enterprises* could unlock trillions in productivity gains.

Startups are racing to develop these agents, while established firms are exploring how to integrate them into operations. Leaders who understand the potential of autonomous organizations will not just improve efficiency—they will rewrite how businesses are structured.

AI Infrastructure and "Picks and Shovels" Businesses

Every gold rush creates opportunities not only for miners but also for those selling picks and shovels. In AI, these include companies building the infrastructure: cloud computing, data labeling services, specialized chips, and compliance platforms. NVIDIA, for instance, became a trillion-dollar company by providing the GPUs that fuel AI systems. The next generation of billion-dollar opportunities may lie in firms solving AI's bottlenecks: data quality, regulation, and ethical oversight.

The Takeaway

AI is not just an efficiency tool—it is a market creator. From drug discovery to climate solutions, from creative industries to autonomous enterprises, the opportunities are vast and accelerating. Billion-dollar markets are already forming, but they will not be evenly distributed. Growth will go to leaders who recognize these openings early, invest boldly, and align innovation with purpose.

The Risks of Ignoring AI Adoption as a Leader

For leaders, choosing not to engage with artificial intelligence is not a neutral decision—it is a high-risk strategy. Just as companies that dismissed electricity or the internet quickly fell behind, organizations that ignore AI adoption today risk irrelevance tomorrow. The cost of inaction compounds over time, creating competitive gaps that are nearly impossible to close.

Falling Behind in Efficiency and Productivity

AI is rapidly becoming the backbone of efficiency across industries. From automating routine tasks to predicting demand with precision, organizations that embrace AI can operate faster, leaner, and smarter. Those that ignore it will face higher costs, slower processes, and reduced margins. Over time, the productivity gap between adopters and laggards widens into a chasm.

Consider manufacturing: factories that integrate AI-driven predictive maintenance minimize downtime and optimize resource use. Competitors without it face equipment failures, higher costs, and longer delays. The leader's refusal to adopt AI is not simply a missed opportunity—it is a direct handicap.

Losing Market Relevance

Markets are being reshaped by AI-enhanced customer expectations. Consumers now anticipate personalization, instant response, and seamless digital experiences—all powered by AI. Leaders who ignore this shift risk appearing outdated and irrelevant.

In retail, companies like Amazon and Alibaba set new standards with AI-driven recommendations, logistics, and customer service. Smaller retailers that fail to adopt similar tools are not just less efficient—they are invisible to customers who now expect intelligent interactions as the norm.

Missed Opportunities for Innovation

AI is not just about doing the same things more efficiently—it enables entirely new products, services, and business models. Ignoring AI means closing the door to innovation that competitors are actively pursuing.

For example, in healthcare, AI enables personalized medicine and predictive diagnostics. Providers who resist adoption may preserve traditional practices but will miss the chance to lead in new markets worth billions. Leaders who fail to see AI as an engine of innovation risk trapping their organizations in a shrinking future.

Increased Risk Exposure

Ironically, ignoring AI can increase risk rather than reduce it. Cybersecurity offers a clear example: attackers are already using AI to develop sophisticated threats. Organizations without AI-driven defenses are leaving themselves dangerously exposed. Similarly, leaders who fail to adopt AI in compliance and monitoring functions may overlook risks that competitors can now detect in real time.

The myth that avoiding AI is "playing it safe" ignores the reality: inaction creates vulnerability.

Talent Drain and Cultural Stagnation

Top talent wants to work where the future is being built. Companies that resist AI adoption send a clear signal: we are not evolving. This drives away innovators, data scientists, and ambitious employees who want to grow their skills in forward-looking environments.

Even beyond talent retention, ignoring AI fosters cultural stagnation. Organizations become risk-averse, resistant to change, and increasingly irrelevant in markets where adaptability is the currency of success.

The Takeaway

The risks of ignoring AI adoption are profound: loss of efficiency, diminished relevance, missed innovation, heightened exposure to threats, and erosion of talent. Leaders cannot treat AI as optional. Choosing not to act is, in fact, a decision—to fall behind. Growth in the AI era requires courage not just to adopt new tools but to reimagine the organization around them. The real risk is not disruption by AI itself, but disruption caused by leaders who refuse to lead with it.

The Next Wave: AI Agents, Generative AI, and Autonomous Enterprises

Artificial intelligence is evolving at a pace that even seasoned leaders find difficult to track. The current wave—driven by generative AI, intelligent agents, and autonomous enterprises—is not just an extension of what came before. It signals a fundamental leap in how organizations will operate, create value, and compete. Leaders who understand this next wave early will shape markets rather than scramble to keep up.

Generative AI: From Automation to Creation

Earlier phases of AI focused on classification, prediction, and optimization. Generative AI adds something profoundly different: creation. Models can now generate text, images, code, music, and video with increasing sophistication. This is more than a technical novelty—it reshapes industries.

- **Media and Marketing**: Campaigns that once required weeks of production can now be generated in minutes.
- **Software Development**: AI coding assistants accelerate programming, enabling faster innovation cycles.
- **Product Design**: AI can generate prototypes, designs, or even new molecules for pharmaceuticals.

Generative AI does not just reduce costs; it expands possibilities. Leaders must now ask: *How do we use AI not just to optimize what exists, but to imagine what doesn't yet exist?*

AI Agents: The Rise of Autonomous Workers

AI agents take automation further by acting autonomously across digital environments. Unlike static scripts, agents can make decisions, adapt to changing inputs, and carry out complex multi-step tasks. Imagine an AI agent that manages procurement end-to-end: identifying suppliers, negotiating contracts, monitoring delivery, and flagging risks—all without human micromanagement.

These agents are early signals of a broader shift: work as we know it will increasingly be performed by networks of humans and autonomous digital colleagues. Leaders who embrace AI agents will discover new efficiencies, while those who resist risk being outpaced by organizations that operate faster and leaner.

Autonomous Enterprises: Organizations That Run Themselves

The convergence of generative AI and AI agents points toward an even bigger leap: autonomous enterprises. These are organizations where core functions—marketing, finance, HR, logistics—are managed by interconnected AI systems with minimal human oversight. Humans shift from running operations to setting vision, ethics, and governance.

This is not science fiction. Early versions are already emerging. Startups are experimenting with AI-managed investment funds, while enterprises are piloting AI-driven supply chains. The direction is clear: the future organization is not just digital—it is autonomous.

Leadership in the Next Wave

The promise of this next wave is immense: faster innovation, reduced costs, and entirely new markets. But so are the challenges. Leaders must:

- **Set boundaries**: Define what decisions AI can make and what must remain human-led.
- **Ensure accountability**: Establish governance frameworks that prevent opaque, unaccountable systems.
- **Reimagine roles**: Prepare employees for work that emphasizes creativity, empathy, and oversight rather than routine tasks.

From Adoption to Reinvention

The critical shift for leaders is this: the first wave of AI adoption was about adding new tools. The next wave is about reinventing entire organizations. Just as electricity didn't just replace gas lamps but enabled whole new industries, AI agents and autonomous enterprises will give rise to business models that today seem unimaginable.

The Takeaway

Generative AI, intelligent agents, and autonomous enterprises mark the next frontier of artificial intelligence. They move AI from a tool of efficiency to a partner in creation, decision-making, and organizational design. Growth will belong to leaders who recognize that the future enterprise is not just AI-enabled but increasingly AI-driven—and who have the courage to reinvent their organizations accordingly.

CHAPTER 3

AI and Leadership: A New Model

Traditional Leadership vs. AI-Enhanced Leadership

Leadership has always been about vision, decision-making, and influence. But the arrival of AI has expanded what it means to lead. Traditional leadership relied heavily on human intuition, experience, and hierarchical authority. AI-enhanced leadership, by contrast, blends human judgment with machine intelligence, shifting the role of leaders from decision owners to decision orchestrators. This difference is not cosmetic—it is transformative.

Traditional Leadership: Experience and Intuition

Historically, leaders were valued for their experience and the ability to make calls in uncertain situations. In business, a seasoned CEO might rely on decades of market knowledge to decide whether to expand into a new region. Data was limited, and leaders often leaned on intuition to fill the gaps.

Traditional leadership emphasized control. Information flowed upward, decisions flowed downward, and authority rested with the person at the top. Success depended on decisiveness, charisma, and consistency in applying proven playbooks.

This model worked in an era where change was slower and information scarcer. But it faces limits in a world defined by real-time data, global complexity, and rapid technological shifts.

AI-Enhanced Leadership: Sense-Making and Augmentation

AI-enhanced leadership recognizes that no leader, no matter how experienced, can match the data-processing power of intelligent systems. Instead of relying solely on intuition, leaders now integrate AI-driven insights into their decision-making. Their role shifts from possessing all the answers to asking the right questions.

For example, an AI system may analyze millions of customer interactions to identify shifting preferences. The AI-enhanced leader does not simply accept or reject the analysis—they interpret it, weigh it against ethical considerations, and align it with long-term vision. They orchestrate the interplay between data and human judgment.

In this model, authority derives less from hierarchy and more from credibility, transparency, and the ability to translate complexity into clarity for teams.

The New Dimensions of Leadership

AI-enhanced leadership expands responsibilities in several ways:

- **From control to empowerment**: Traditional leaders focused on directing teams; AI leaders design systems where humans and AI collaborate, freeing people to focus on creativity and innovation.
- **From intuition to evidence-based foresight**: While intuition still matters, leaders now rely on predictive analytics to anticipate market shifts before they happen.
- **From static playbooks to adaptive strategy**: Traditional leadership often reused strategies that worked in the past. AI-enhanced leaders adapt continuously, informed by live data and scenario modeling.
- **From isolated decisions to systemic thinking**: Leaders must now understand not just the immediate impact of choices but also how AI-driven changes ripple across ecosystems and societies.

Case in Point: Retail Transformation

In traditional retail, leaders relied on experience and seasonal trends to plan inventory. Today, AI-enhanced leadership means using predictive models that forecast demand at a granular level—by product, region, and even customer segment. Leaders are not replaced; they are elevated. Instead of guessing which products will sell, they focus on designing supply chains, partnerships, and customer experiences that align with predictive insights.

The difference is not in whether leaders make decisions, but in *how* they make them and *what* they prioritize.

The Takeaway

Traditional leadership thrived in a world of limited data and slower change. AI-enhanced leadership thrives in a world of abundant data and constant disruption. The role of the leader has shifted from being the ultimate source of answers to being the ultimate integrator of insights. Growth now depends on leaders who embrace AI not as a threat to authority but as an amplifier of vision, strategy, and impact.

Leading Human–AI Collaboration (Man + Machine Teams)

The future of work is not about humans competing against machines—it is about humans and machines working together. AI systems excel at processing massive datasets, identifying patterns, and automating repetitive tasks. Humans excel at empathy, creativity, and ethical reasoning. The most effective leaders in the AI era are those who know how to design and lead teams where man and machine complement each other, amplifying strengths while minimizing weaknesses.

The Shift from Replacement to Augmentation

The dominant fear around AI is replacement: jobs lost, roles automated, skills made obsolete. While automation is real, the deeper truth is that AI augments human capability when guided effectively. For example, radiologists once feared being replaced by AI diagnostic systems. Instead, AI now acts as a second set of eyes, improving accuracy and allowing doctors to focus more on patient care. The job did not disappear—it evolved.

Leaders play a critical role in reframing the narrative from *replacement* to *augmentation*. This requires not just deploying AI but communicating clearly how it enhances human work.

Designing Human–AI Teams

Leading man + machine teams requires intentional design. Leaders must answer three questions:

1. **What should AI do best?** Tasks that involve scale, repetition, or prediction.
2. **What should humans do best?** Tasks that involve judgment, empathy, and creative problem-solving.
3. **How should they interact?** Designing workflows where AI provides insights and automation, while humans validate, adapt, and contextualize.

Consider customer service: AI chatbots handle simple, repetitive queries, while human agents step in for complex or emotionally sensitive issues. Leaders who design this balance well deliver both efficiency and empathy.

Building Trust in Human–AI Collaboration

For collaboration to succeed, both employees and customers must trust AI systems. If employees believe AI is a competitor rather than a partner, resistance will grow. Leaders must invest in transparency—explaining how AI works, where it adds value, and where humans remain essential.

Take aviation: pilots trust autopilot systems not because they surrender control, but because they understand when and how those systems are used. Similarly, employees must see AI as a reliable teammate rather than a black box. Leaders foster trust by ensuring explainability, training, and open communication.

The New Skillset for Leaders

Leading human–AI teams requires a different skillset than traditional management:

- **System thinking**: Understanding how workflows evolve when machines take on parts of the process.
- **Empathy**: Supporting employees through the transition and helping them see opportunities for growth.
- **Digital fluency**: Not needing to code, but being able to interpret AI outputs and challenge them when necessary.
- **Change leadership**: Managing fear, building buy-in, and cultivating a culture where experimentation with AI is encouraged.

Case Study: Financial Services

In wealth management, AI can generate investment recommendations tailored to clients. Human advisors, however, remain indispensable for explaining strategies, managing client emotions, and aligning investments with life goals. Firms that tried to replace advisors with robo-advisors entirely struggled with adoption. Firms that blended AI insights with human relationships created new value at scale.

The Takeaway

Human–AI collaboration is the defining feature of the new workplace. Leaders who succeed will not pit man against machine but will design partnerships where both excel. Growth comes from integration: letting AI handle what it does best, empowering humans to do what only they can, and building trust so that the team—human and machine together—operates at its highest potential.

Building Trust and Credibility in a Data-Driven World

In the AI era, trust is not a soft value—it is a strategic asset. As organizations increasingly rely on algorithms to guide decisions, employees, customers, and stakeholders demand confidence that those systems are reliable, fair, and transparent. Leaders must recognize that their credibility now depends not only on personal integrity but also on how responsibly they use data and AI.

Why Trust Matters More Than Ever

AI-driven decisions affect lives in ways that are immediate and personal: approving loans, diagnosing diseases, screening job candidates. When people feel those systems are biased or opaque, they lose trust—not just in the technology, but in the organization deploying it.

Consider a hiring platform that inadvertently favors certain demographics because of biased training data. Even if unintentional, the fallout is reputational damage, legal risk, and a loss of employee morale. Trust erodes faster in the digital era because skepticism spreads instantly across social media and networks.

Transparency as a Leadership Imperative

Traditional leadership relied on authority and track record to build credibility. In the AI era, transparency is essential. Leaders must ensure systems are explainable—employees and customers need to know *why* a decision was made, not just the outcome.

For example, when a bank denies a loan application, telling the applicant simply that "the system decided" is unacceptable. AI-enhanced leadership means demanding that algorithms provide human-readable explanations. This transparency protects trust, even when the outcome is unfavorable.

Balancing Data Power with Responsibility

Leaders now wield unprecedented access to data: consumer behavior, employee productivity, financial trends, and more. But with power comes responsibility. Misuse of data—whether through invasive surveillance, hidden biases, or weak privacy protections—undermines credibility.

Apple has built its brand partly on data privacy, positioning itself as a trusted guardian of customer information. That trust translates into loyalty and differentiation. Leaders in any industry can learn from this: safeguarding data is not just compliance, it is strategy.

Building Internal Trust with Employees

Trust is equally critical inside the organization. Employees must believe that AI is being used to support their work, not to monitor or replace them unfairly. Leaders should:

- **Communicate openly** about how AI is deployed.
- **Include employees in design and feedback** so they feel ownership, not surveillance.
- **Invest in reskilling** so AI adoption signals opportunity, not obsolescence.

Without internal trust, AI initiatives face resistance, slow adoption, and hidden sabotage.

The Role of Ethical Consistency

Credibility is not built on isolated gestures but on consistent choices. Leaders who speak about fairness but deploy opaque, biased AI systems create cynicism. By contrast, leaders who prioritize fairness in AI—even at short-term cost—earn lasting credibility.

For example, some financial institutions have voluntarily limited the use of certain AI systems in lending until bias issues were resolved. This slowed immediate rollout but strengthened long-term trust with regulators and customers.

The Takeaway

In a data-driven world, leadership credibility depends on more than vision and execution—it depends on trust. Transparency, ethical consistency, and responsible data use are not optional add-ons; they are the foundation of sustainable growth. Leaders who fail to earn trust will find their organizations questioned at every step. Leaders who build it will create resilience, loyalty, and influence in an era where data and AI touch every human decision.

The Four Pillars of AI Leadership: Vision, Strategy, Ethics, Adaptability

Artificial intelligence is changing the very definition of leadership. To thrive, leaders must go beyond adopting tools—they must build organizations that can evolve with them. Four pillars form the foundation of AI leadership: vision, strategy, ethics, and adaptability. Together, they provide the compass leaders need to navigate a future shaped by both human judgment and machine intelligence.

Vision: Seeing Beyond the Horizon

AI leaders are not defined by their ability to manage technology but by their ability to imagine possibilities others cannot yet see. Vision means asking: *How will AI reshape our industry, our customers' expectations, and our role in society?*

For example, when Jensen Huang of NVIDIA envisioned GPUs not just as graphics processors but as engines for AI, he positioned the company at the center of a trillion-dollar revolution. Leaders with vision don't wait for consensus—they anticipate the future and guide others toward it.

Strategy: Turning Potential into Action

Vision without execution is imagination. Strategy turns vision into measurable progress. In the AI era, this means:

- Identifying where AI can create the most value in the organization.
- Prioritizing investments based on impact and feasibility.
- Scaling from pilots to enterprise-wide adoption.

Leaders must avoid the trap of endless experimentation with no integration. A clear strategy ensures AI is not scattered across isolated projects but embedded in the core of the business model.

Consider how Netflix used AI strategically—not only for recommendations but across operations, from content creation to bandwidth optimization. This holistic approach made AI central to its business, not just an experiment.

Ethics: Guiding Innovation with Responsibility

As AI expands its reach, ethical considerations are no longer optional—they are leadership imperatives. Leaders must ensure systems are fair, transparent, and aligned with human values. This means addressing questions like:

- Is the data representative and unbiased?
- Are customers' privacy and autonomy protected?
- Do employees trust that AI is being used to empower, not exploit?

Failing on ethics is not just a moral lapse—it's a strategic failure. Scandals around biased AI or privacy breaches erode trust, invite regulation, and damage brands. By contrast, companies that lead with ethical integrity build resilience and long-term loyalty.

Adaptability: Thriving in Constant Change

Perhaps the most overlooked pillar is adaptability. AI evolves at breakneck speed—what is cutting-edge today may be obsolete in a year. Leaders must build cultures of continuous learning and agility. This means:

- Encouraging experimentation and learning from failure.
- Updating strategies as technology and markets shift.
- Reskilling employees to grow with the organization.

Adaptability separates organizations that flourish from those that falter. Kodak once dominated photography but failed to adapt to digital disruption. Leaders in the AI era cannot afford the same mistake.

The Takeaway

Vision, strategy, ethics, and adaptability form the core of AI leadership. Vision defines the destination. Strategy charts the path. Ethics ensures the journey builds trust. Adaptability keeps the organization moving forward as the landscape shifts. Growth in the AI era will not come from leaders who focus on technology alone but from those who balance foresight with responsibility and agility.

Case Study: How Forward-Thinking Leaders Outperformed by Embracing AI Early

Abstract theories about AI leadership are important, but nothing illustrates the stakes better than real-world examples. Across industries, forward-thinking leaders who embraced AI early gained decisive advantages—while those who hesitated fell behind. These case studies show how vision, strategy, ethics, and adaptability translate into measurable performance.

Microsoft: Betting Early on AI Integration

When Satya Nadella took over as CEO in 2014, Microsoft was losing ground in consumer tech. Instead of trying to compete head-to-head with Apple or Google in devices, Nadella doubled down on cloud computing and AI. Under his leadership, Microsoft integrated AI into its core products—Office 365, Azure, and Teams—while also investing heavily in generative AI partnerships.

The result: Microsoft redefined itself as an AI-first enterprise platform, creating sticky ecosystems that power businesses globally. Early adoption allowed the company to capture enterprise trust and secure its place as a leader in the AI revolution.

Netflix: Reinventing Entertainment with AI

Netflix began as a DVD rental company. Its leaders recognized early that data and AI could redefine entertainment. By using algorithms to personalize recommendations, predict viewing patterns, and even inform content production, Netflix transformed not just its own business but the entire media landscape.

Competitors that stuck to traditional broadcast models struggled, while Netflix leveraged AI to scale globally. Today, personalization is the standard in streaming—but Netflix gained years of advantage by pioneering it early.

Tesla: AI as the Core of the Business Model

Elon Musk positioned Tesla not merely as an electric car company but as a software-driven AI company on wheels. By investing in autonomous driving systems, Tesla reframed the value proposition of automobiles—from transportation to mobility-as-a-service.

While traditional automakers hesitated, Tesla's early AI adoption created a powerful feedback loop: millions of cars feeding data into AI models, continuously improving performance. This early move gave Tesla not just a technological edge but also brand dominance as the company synonymous with the future of mobility.

Healthcare: AI in Early Diagnostics

In healthcare, leaders at institutions like Mayo Clinic embraced AI for diagnostics early on, integrating systems that detect cancer and heart disease at stages earlier than human clinicians could. By positioning AI as a partner rather than a replacement for doctors, they improved patient outcomes and established themselves as leaders in medical innovation.

Hospitals that delayed AI adoption now find themselves struggling to catch up—not only in outcomes but also in attracting top talent who want to work where innovation is thriving.

Lessons for Leaders

These cases reveal consistent patterns:

- **Early adopters compound advantage**: The more data AI systems process, the smarter they become. Latecomers face a steeper climb.

- **AI is not an add-on—it's a redefinition**: The most successful leaders wove AI into the fabric of their business, not just as a side project.
- **Culture matters**: Organizations that embraced experimentation and learning thrived. Those that clung to old playbooks stagnated.

The Takeaway

Forward-thinking leaders who embraced AI early outperformed by turning disruption into opportunity. They didn't wait for perfect clarity—they acted with vision, strategy, ethics, and adaptability. Their success is proof that in the AI era, leadership is not about waiting until the path is safe. It is about moving early enough to shape the path itself.

CHAPTER 4

Building AI-Ready Teams

Identifying Skill Gaps in Your Workforce

AI adoption does not begin with technology—it begins with people. A leader's first responsibility in building an AI-ready team is understanding where their workforce stands today and what skills will be needed tomorrow. Identifying skill gaps is not about pointing out deficiencies; it is about mapping potential and preparing employees to thrive in the digital era.

Why Skill Gaps Matter

AI is not a single tool but a collection of capabilities—data analysis, machine learning, automation, and generative systems. Each of these reshapes workflows differently. Without the right skills, organizations risk underutilizing AI, mismanaging its deployment, or leaving employees behind. Skill gaps, if ignored, become barriers to adoption and innovation.

For example, a financial services firm may deploy AI for fraud detection. If employees lack data literacy, they may distrust the outputs, misinterpret the insights, or fail to act on them effectively. The technology then becomes underused—not because it lacks power, but because the workforce lacks readiness.

Mapping Current Capabilities

The first step is to conduct a skills audit. Leaders should assess employees across three dimensions:

1. **Technical literacy** – Do employees understand how to use AI tools in their daily work?
2. **Data literacy** – Can teams interpret AI outputs, question assumptions, and make informed decisions?
3. **Soft skills** – Are employees prepared for roles requiring adaptability, collaboration with AI, and creative problem-solving?

Surveys, interviews, and performance reviews can provide insights, but the most effective leaders go further—embedding AI pilots and observing how teams adapt in practice.

Future-Focused Gap Analysis

Identifying skill gaps is not just about the present. Leaders must anticipate where their industry is heading. For example:

- **Healthcare**: A growing need for professionals who can interpret AI-driven diagnostics.
- **Logistics**: Skills in managing AI-powered supply chain systems.
- **Education**: Teachers who can integrate AI tutoring platforms into classrooms.

By comparing current workforce skills with future industry demands, leaders can identify not just today's gaps but tomorrow's opportunities.

Engaging Employees in the Process

Skill gap analysis should not feel like a judgment imposed from the top. Leaders who succeed make it participatory. They involve employees in self-assessments, open discussions, and career planning. This fosters trust and shifts the narrative from *AI as a threat* to *AI as a growth pathway*.

For example, when AT&T recognized looming skill gaps in its workforce, it launched a massive reskilling initiative where employees could choose new learning tracks aligned with future roles. By framing it as empowerment rather than evaluation, the company built buy-in and momentum.

The Hidden Gaps: Culture and Mindset

Beyond technical skills, leaders must identify cultural gaps. Does the organization reward experimentation, or punish failure? Do employees see AI as a partner or as a competitor? Often, the biggest barriers are not technical at all but cultural. Leaders who overlook this dimension risk investing in training without addressing resistance.

The Takeaway

Identifying skill gaps is the foundation of building AI-ready teams. It requires a clear-eyed view of current capabilities, a forward-looking analysis of industry trends, and an honest assessment of cultural readiness. Growth in the AI era is not just about acquiring technology—it is about ensuring people have the skills and confidence to use it. Leaders who invest in this step set the stage for a workforce that thrives rather than struggles in the age of intelligent machines.

Upskilling and Reskilling Employees for the AI Era

Once leaders identify skill gaps, the next step is to close them. In the AI era, this means building a workforce that is not only technically competent but also adaptable. Upskilling and reskilling are no longer optional HR initiatives—they are strategic imperatives that determine whether organizations can evolve or fall behind.

The Difference Between Upskilling and Reskilling

- **Upskilling** equips employees with new capabilities to enhance their current roles. For example, a marketer might learn to use generative AI tools to design campaigns more efficiently.
- **Reskilling** prepares employees for entirely new roles created by technological change. For instance, a factory worker whose tasks are automated may retrain as a data technician overseeing AI-powered machinery.

Both approaches are critical. Upskilling keeps teams competitive in the short term, while reskilling ensures long-term relevance as industries evolve.

Why AI Makes This Urgent

The half-life of skills is shrinking dramatically. According to research, technical skills can become outdated in as little as two to three years. AI accelerates this cycle. Leaders cannot assume that past expertise guarantees future success. Investing in learning is now as important as investing in technology.

Companies that wait until disruption arrives will face talent shortages and employee anxiety. Those that act early create confidence, loyalty, and competitive advantage.

Practical Approaches to Upskilling and Reskilling

1. **Modular Learning Programs**: Instead of long, one-off training sessions, organizations should offer bite-sized, continuous learning modules. Employees can learn AI basics, data literacy, or tool-specific skills in ways that fit into their work schedules.

2. **On-the-Job Experimentation**: Learning is most effective when applied. Leaders should create safe environments where employees can experiment with AI tools without fear of failure.
3. **Partnerships with Education Providers**: Collaborations with universities, online platforms, and certification programs give employees access to cutting-edge AI knowledge.
4. **Mentorship and Peer Learning**: Pairing tech-savvy employees with those less familiar creates organic knowledge transfer.
5. **Career Pathway Transparency**: Employees need clarity on how upskilling or reskilling will impact their future. If a data-entry role is being automated, leaders must show the new opportunities available after training.

Case Study: Amazon's $700 Million Reskilling Initiative

Amazon recognized that automation and AI would transform its workforce of over 750,000 employees. Instead of waiting for displacement to occur, it launched a $700 million reskilling program, offering training in fields like cloud computing, data science, and machine learning. The message was clear: AI may change roles, but the company is committed to ensuring employees evolve with it. This proactive investment not only protected Amazon's talent base but also reinforced employee trust.

The Role of Leadership in Driving Learning

Upskilling and reskilling are not simply HR's responsibility. Leaders must:

- Set the tone by emphasizing continuous learning as a cultural norm.
- Allocate budget and time for training, signaling that it is a priority.
- Lead by example, showing willingness to learn and adapt alongside employees.

The Takeaway

In the AI era, the organizations that thrive will be those that invest as much in people as in technology. Upskilling and reskilling are not side projects—they are the backbone of resilience. Growth comes from preparing employees not just to survive disruption but to seize the opportunities it creates. Leaders who commit to this investment build teams that are not only AI-ready but future-proof.

Fostering a Culture of Innovation and Adaptability

Technology adoption is not only a technical challenge—it is a cultural one. An organization may invest millions in AI tools, but without a culture that embraces experimentation, collaboration, and adaptability, those tools remain underused. Leaders in the AI era must therefore focus not just on skill-building but on shaping a culture where innovation becomes second nature.

Why Culture Matters in the AI Era

AI changes the pace of business. Strategies that once evolved over years now pivot in months. In this environment, rigid cultures collapse under pressure. A culture of innovation and adaptability ensures employees are not paralyzed by change but energized by it.

Consider the contrast between Kodak and Adobe. Kodak clung to its traditional film business, resisting digital innovation until it was too late. Adobe, by contrast, embraced digital disruption early, reinventing itself with cloud-based creative tools and, more recently, AI-powered design features. The difference was not only technological foresight but cultural openness to reinvention.

Building Psychological Safety

Innovation thrives where employees feel safe to take risks. Leaders must create environments where experimentation is rewarded, not punished. This means shifting the narrative from *failure as weakness* to *failure as learning.*

For example, Google's "20% time" policy encouraged employees to spend part of their workweek on personal projects. While not every idea succeeded, many innovations—including Gmail—emerged from this culture of safe experimentation. Leaders in the AI era can apply the same principle by giving teams room to explore AI tools creatively without fear of judgment.

Encouraging Cross-Functional Collaboration

AI impacts every corner of an organization, from HR to marketing to operations. To unlock its full potential, leaders must break down silos. Cross-functional teams—where technologists, business strategists, and creatives collaborate—generate insights no single group could achieve alone.

For example, in healthcare, effective AI adoption often comes from collaboration between clinicians, data scientists, and ethicists. This diversity of perspectives ensures the technology is not only accurate but also practical and ethical in real-world use.

Rewarding Curiosity and Continuous Learning

An adaptable culture celebrates curiosity. Leaders can foster this by:

- Recognizing employees who proactively learn new tools.
- Sharing success stories of teams that leveraged AI to solve problems.
- Providing platforms for employees to showcase innovative ideas.

When curiosity is rewarded, innovation becomes contagious. Employees shift from fearing disruption to seeking opportunities.

Leading by Example

Culture begins at the top. Leaders who experiment with AI tools themselves send a powerful signal. When executives openly share how they are learning and adapting, it normalizes the idea that no one is above change. This humility fosters trust and motivates teams to embrace new ways of working.

The Takeaway

Fostering a culture of innovation and adaptability is essential for AI readiness. Skills alone are insufficient if the environment discourages risk-taking or clings to outdated methods. Leaders who build psychological safety, encourage collaboration, reward curiosity, and model adaptability create organizations that thrive in uncertainty. Growth in the AI era is not just about adopting technology—it is about cultivating the mindset that turns technology into transformation.

Managing Resistance and Fear of Job Loss

AI adoption is as much an emotional journey as it is a technical one. While leaders may see opportunity in automation, employees often see uncertainty—and with it, fear of job loss. Left unaddressed, this resistance can stall projects, create mistrust, and undermine cultural momentum. Effective AI leaders confront these fears head-on, guiding their teams with empathy, clarity, and opportunity.

Why Fear Arises

The fear of being replaced by machines is not irrational. History shows that technological revolutions—from the industrial age to the computer era—have displaced certain roles. What is often overlooked, however, is that new roles always emerge. The challenge is not whether jobs will change, but whether leaders will prepare their people for the transition.

Employees fear AI for three main reasons:

1. **Loss of relevance** – Will their skills still matter?
2. **Lack of control** – Will machines make decisions they once owned?
3. **Uncertainty about the future** – Will new opportunities be accessible to them?

Transparency as the First Line of Defense

The worst response to fear is silence. When leaders deploy AI without explanation, rumors fill the void. Transparency is essential: leaders should explain not only what AI is being introduced but why, how it will be used, and what it means for employees' roles.

For example, when a European bank rolled out AI tools in its back-office operations, leadership hosted town halls and Q&A sessions where employees could voice concerns. By addressing fears directly, they built trust and reduced resistance.

Reframing the Narrative: From Threat to Opportunity

Fear often stems from framing. If AI is presented solely as a cost-cutting measure, employees will naturally assume their jobs are at risk. Leaders must reframe AI as a tool for empowerment: reducing repetitive tasks, freeing up time for creative work, and opening new career paths.

In healthcare, some hospitals introduced AI to handle administrative paperwork, which initially worried nurses. Leadership reframed the shift by highlighting how it would give nurses more time with patients. Once staff experienced the change, fear gave way to appreciation.

Creating Pathways to Growth

Managing fear is not just about communication—it requires action. Leaders must provide concrete pathways for employees to grow with AI, such as:

- **Reskilling programs** for roles most at risk.
- **Upskilling initiatives** for employees to use AI tools directly.
- **Internal mobility opportunities** so employees see tangible futures within the organization.

For example, AT&T launched retraining initiatives where employees could choose future career paths supported by company-funded learning. This approach turned fear into agency.

Engaging Employees in Design

Another way to reduce resistance is to involve employees in shaping AI adoption. When workers participate in testing tools, providing feedback, and suggesting improvements, they feel ownership rather than displacement. Leaders who co-create AI strategies with their teams build advocates instead of adversaries.

The Takeaway

Managing resistance and fear of job loss is a central responsibility of AI leaders. Transparency, reframing, growth pathways, and employee engagement transform fear into trust. Growth in the AI era is not about minimizing disruption—it is about leading people through it with empathy and vision. Leaders who succeed in this task build not only AI-ready teams but also resilient, loyal organizations prepared for the future.

Using AI Tools for Recruitment, Onboarding, and Team Development

Building AI-ready teams does not stop at training current employees—it starts with how new talent is identified, welcomed, and developed. Recruitment, onboarding, and team development are three areas where AI is already reshaping leadership practices. Leaders who leverage these tools wisely gain a competitive edge in attracting, integrating, and nurturing the workforce of the future.

Smarter Recruitment with AI

Hiring has long been one of the most resource-intensive and error-prone leadership tasks. Traditional processes rely heavily on resumes, human judgment, and limited data points. AI changes this by analyzing vast pools of candidates and identifying matches based on skills, experience, and cultural fit.

For example:

- **Resume screening tools** can filter thousands of applications in minutes, reducing bias by focusing on skills rather than surface-level markers.
- **Predictive analytics** can forecast which candidates are likely to succeed in specific roles based on historical data.

- **Chatbots** can engage applicants at scale, answering questions and keeping them engaged throughout the process.

However, leaders must ensure these tools are used responsibly. AI can reinforce biases if not monitored carefully. A leader's role is to demand transparency in the algorithms and pair machine-driven insights with human judgment.

AI in Onboarding: Creating Seamless Integration

The onboarding experience sets the tone for an employee's relationship with an organization. AI can personalize and streamline this critical stage:

- **Virtual assistants** guide new hires through paperwork, training modules, and policy questions.
- **Adaptive learning platforms** tailor onboarding content to each individual's background, allowing faster ramp-up times.
- **Analytics** track engagement, helping leaders spot when new employees may feel disconnected.

This creates a smoother experience for employees while reducing administrative burdens on HR teams. Leaders who use AI in onboarding signal that their organizations are forward-looking and employee-centered.

Team Development with AI Insights

Once employees are integrated, leaders face the ongoing challenge of developing teams. AI provides powerful tools for this as well:

- **Performance analytics** help leaders identify strengths and gaps within teams.
- **Collaboration tools** analyze communication patterns to reveal bottlenecks or opportunities for better coordination.

- **Personalized learning platforms** continuously upskill employees, aligning development with both individual goals and organizational needs.

For example, some organizations use AI to identify high-potential employees by analyzing patterns in project performance, peer feedback, and learning engagement. Leaders can then design targeted development programs, ensuring talent is nurtured and retained.

Balancing Technology with Human Leadership

While AI can accelerate recruitment, onboarding, and development, leaders must remember that these processes are deeply human experiences. Candidates want to feel valued, new hires want to feel welcomed, and employees want to feel supported in their growth. AI should handle scale and personalization, but leaders must provide empathy, mentorship, and vision.

A chatbot may answer questions quickly, but only a leader can inspire a new employee with purpose. An algorithm may flag skill gaps, but only a leader can have the career conversation that motivates growth. AI provides the data; leadership provides the meaning.

The Takeaway

AI is transforming how organizations attract, integrate, and develop talent. Used responsibly, it reduces bias in hiring, personalizes onboarding, and accelerates employee growth. But the true advantage comes when leaders combine these tools with human connection. Growth in the AI era will not come from automating people processes but from using AI to amplify the most human aspects of leadership: trust, empathy, and inspiration.

CHAPTER 5

The AI Leader's Toolkit

Productivity AI Tools Every Leader Should Know

In the AI era, productivity is no longer defined simply by time management or process optimization. Intelligent tools now give leaders the ability to automate tasks, generate insights, and make better decisions at scale. Knowing which tools to use—and how to use them—can mean the difference between an organization that lags and one that thrives. The most effective leaders don't just adopt AI tools; they integrate them into daily leadership practices.

Automation for Administrative Efficiency

Administrative work consumes a significant portion of leaders' time. AI-driven automation tools now handle tasks such as scheduling, expense management, and document processing.

- **Scheduling assistants** like x.ai or Calendly (with AI enhancements) automatically manage calendars, rescheduling conflicts without back-and-forth emails.
- **Expense automation** tools scan receipts, categorize expenses, and flag anomalies instantly.
- **Document automation** systems draft contracts, generate reports, and summarize meeting notes.

By offloading these repetitive tasks, leaders gain back hours each week—time that can be reinvested in strategic thinking and team engagement.

AI for Decision Support

Leaders make countless decisions daily, many of which require rapid access to accurate information. Decision-support AI tools analyze large datasets and present actionable insights.

- **Business intelligence platforms** like Tableau and Power BI now integrate AI to surface trends leaders might miss.
- **Scenario modeling tools** simulate outcomes, helping leaders anticipate risks and opportunities.
- **AI-driven dashboards** consolidate real-time data across finance, operations, and customer metrics.

Instead of drowning in information, leaders can focus on interpreting insights and aligning them with organizational goals.

Generative AI for Content and Communication

Communication is central to leadership, and generative AI has become a powerful ally:

- **Writing assistants** like ChatGPT or Jasper help draft speeches, memos, and reports.
- **Presentation tools** generate slides, visuals, and storyboards tailored to an audience.
- **Translation tools** break down language barriers, making global collaboration seamless.

The key is not to outsource leadership communication entirely, but to use AI as a partner—accelerating creation while preserving authenticity.

AI for Personal Productivity

Leaders also benefit from AI tools that enhance personal productivity and learning:

- **Focus tools** track attention and suggest ways to minimize distraction.
- **AI coaching platforms** analyze leadership styles and provide personalized feedback.
- **Learning companions** recommend books, articles, or courses based on leadership goals.

These tools transform personal development from sporadic to continuous, enabling leaders to grow alongside their organizations.

The Leadership Mindset for Productivity AI

Having access to tools is not enough. Leaders must:

1. **Curate intentionally** – Focus on tools that solve real pain points, not just the newest trend.
2. **Model usage** – When leaders use AI tools visibly, teams are more likely to adopt them.
3. **Balance efficiency with empathy** – Productivity should free leaders to deepen human connections, not avoid them.

The Takeaway

AI productivity tools are not about replacing leadership—they are about amplifying it. From automation to decision support, from communication to personal growth, these tools free leaders from low-value tasks and empower them to focus on what matters most: vision, strategy, and people. Growth in the AI era requires leaders to master not just the art of leadership but the toolkit that makes leadership scalable.

AI Agents for Business: How Autonomous Tools Change Operations

The next wave of AI adoption is being driven by **AI agents**—autonomous digital tools that can perform complex tasks across multiple systems without constant human oversight. Unlike traditional software, which follows predefined rules, AI agents can adapt, learn, and make decisions in real time. For leaders, this represents both a massive opportunity and a new challenge: how to design organizations that integrate human talent with autonomous digital colleagues.

What Makes AI Agents Different

Traditional automation handles repetitive tasks—think of robotic process automation (RPA) that processes invoices or schedules reports. AI agents go further. They can:

- Work across different applications, from email to CRM to financial systems.
- Interpret natural language instructions and act on them.
- Adapt to changing inputs, making decisions dynamically.
- Execute multi-step processes without constant human approval.

For example, an AI agent could handle procurement end-to-end: identifying suppliers, negotiating terms, processing orders, and monitoring delivery—tasks that once required multiple employees.

Transforming Business Operations

AI agents are beginning to reshape operations across industries:

- **Customer Service**: Beyond chatbots, AI agents can resolve billing issues, escalate cases, and even anticipate customer needs based on past behavior.
- **Finance**: Agents can close books, reconcile accounts, and flag anomalies in real time.
- **Marketing**: Autonomous agents can design campaigns, run A/B tests, and adjust budgets dynamically.
- **Supply Chains**: Agents can monitor inventory, predict demand, and automatically trigger replenishment.

The result is not just efficiency but resilience—organizations that can operate continuously, flexibly, and with fewer bottlenecks.

The Leadership Challenge: Control vs. Autonomy

AI agents raise a critical leadership question: how much autonomy should they have? While delegating routine tasks to agents unlocks speed, leaders must ensure transparency and accountability. Blind trust in autonomous systems can expose organizations to ethical risks, regulatory breaches, or reputational harm.

Leaders should establish **clear boundaries**:

- What decisions can agents make independently?
- What requires human validation?
- How are outcomes monitored and audited?

The right balance ensures efficiency without losing oversight.

Case Study: Autonomous Marketing Agents

A global e-commerce firm tested AI agents to manage digital advertising. Instead of marketing managers manually adjusting bids and budgets, agents ran campaigns autonomously, optimizing in real time. The result: a 25% improvement in ROI and faster adaptation to shifting consumer behavior. Human marketers were not eliminated; they shifted focus to creative strategy, brand storytelling, and long-term planning.

This illustrates the principle of **augmentation, not replacement**. Agents took over execution; humans elevated their focus.

Preparing Teams for AI Agents

Introducing AI agents requires cultural readiness. Employees may fear being sidelined if agents take on core tasks. Leaders must:

- Communicate clearly how agents will support, not replace, human roles.

- Reskill teams for higher-value work, such as oversight and innovation.
- Involve employees in shaping workflows that integrate agents.

The Takeaway

AI agents are more than tools—they are digital colleagues that change how organizations operate. They bring unprecedented efficiency and flexibility, but they also challenge leaders to rethink autonomy, accountability, and team dynamics. Growth in the AI era will belong to leaders who embrace AI agents as partners, balancing speed and innovation with trust and responsibility.

Data Dashboards and Decision Support Systems

Leadership in the AI era is inseparable from data. But raw data alone does not create value—it overwhelms. The true power lies in turning streams of information into insights leaders can act on. That's where AI-powered dashboards and decision support systems come in. They provide clarity in complexity, allowing leaders to make faster, smarter, and more confident choices.

From Reports to Real-Time Insight

Traditional reporting delivers static snapshots—weekly sales reports, quarterly financial summaries, annual customer surveys. By the time data is compiled, it's often outdated. AI-powered dashboards replace lagging indicators with **real-time insights**, drawing from live data sources across operations.

For example:

- A retail leader can see sales performance by product, region, and channel instantly, with predictive forecasts for the next quarter.
- A logistics leader can monitor fleet movements in real time, with AI suggesting optimal routes to reduce delays.

This shift from reactive to proactive decision-making fundamentally changes how leaders steer organizations.

The Role of Decision Support Systems

Decision support systems (DSS) go beyond dashboards by not only presenting data but also recommending actions. They use AI models to simulate scenarios, highlight risks, and rank potential choices.

For instance, a CFO evaluating expansion into a new market might use a DSS to model different outcomes based on exchange rates, regulatory changes, and customer demand. The system doesn't replace judgment—it enhances it by surfacing possibilities humans may not see.

Benefits for Leaders

1. **Clarity in Complexity** – AI simplifies vast datasets into clear visuals and recommendations.
2. **Faster Response Times** – Real-time alerts let leaders act before small issues escalate into crises.
3. **Data-Driven Credibility** – Decisions backed by transparent data earn more trust from boards, teams, and investors.
4. **Strategic Foresight** – Predictive analytics move leaders from hindsight to foresight.

Pitfalls to Avoid

While dashboards and DSS are powerful, leaders must guard against overreliance:

- **Data without context**: AI can surface correlations that lack strategic meaning.
- **Black box risks**: If leaders can't explain why a recommendation was made, credibility erodes.
- **Analysis paralysis**: Too much data, even well-visualized, can still overwhelm unless priorities are clear.

The leader's role is to ensure systems provide not just data, but decision-enabling clarity.

Case Study: AI Dashboards in Healthcare

A hospital network implemented AI dashboards to monitor patient flow, bed capacity, and staffing levels. Leaders gained real-time visibility into bottlenecks and could reallocate resources instantly. During COVID-19 surges, these tools proved invaluable—allowing proactive decisions that saved lives. Importantly, human oversight ensured ethical allocation of limited resources.

The Takeaway

AI-powered dashboards and decision support systems transform leadership from reactive to proactive. They turn overwhelming data into actionable clarity, empowering leaders to act with speed and confidence. Growth in the AI era depends not on having more information, but on harnessing it wisely—and ensuring that human judgment remains at the center of every decision.

AI for Communication: Chatbots, Assistants, and Personalization

Communication is the lifeblood of leadership. How leaders connect with employees, customers, and stakeholders determines trust, loyalty, and influence. In the AI era, communication is being reshaped by intelligent tools—chatbots, virtual assistants, and personalization engines—that extend leaders' reach and responsiveness while transforming how organizations interact with people.

Chatbots: Scaling Conversations

Chatbots have evolved far beyond scripted FAQ tools. Powered by natural language processing, modern chatbots can handle complex interactions, understand intent, and learn from past conversations. For leaders, this means:

- **Customer engagement at scale** – Chatbots answer queries instantly, reducing wait times and improving satisfaction.
- **Employee support** – Internal bots guide staff through HR processes, IT troubleshooting, or training resources.
- **Data collection** – Conversations generate insights into customer pain points and employee needs.

Leaders must ensure, however, that chatbots are designed with empathy. When poorly implemented, they frustrate rather than help. The best leaders balance automation with the option for human escalation when needed.

Virtual Assistants: Extending Leadership Bandwidth

AI-powered assistants such as Microsoft Copilot or Google Assistant are redefining personal productivity. They schedule meetings, draft emails, summarize documents, and even generate presentations. For leaders managing heavy communication demands, these assistants act as amplifiers.

The advantage is not just efficiency—it is presence. By delegating routine communication tasks to assistants, leaders gain more time for meaningful conversations with their teams and stakeholders.

Personalization: Making Communication Human Again

Ironically, AI makes large-scale communication feel more personal. Personalization engines analyze data to tailor messages, recommendations, and experiences to individuals.

- **Customer communication**: Personalized product suggestions or service updates increase engagement and loyalty.
- **Employee communication**: Leaders can tailor development opportunities, wellness initiatives, or recognition programs to individual preferences.

For example, LinkedIn uses AI to personalize job recommendations and learning suggestions, enhancing user engagement. Leaders can apply similar principles internally, making employees feel seen and valued.

The Leadership Imperative: Authenticity

AI can draft emails, generate speeches, or even simulate voices. But the risk is losing authenticity. Communication is not just about words—it's about trust. Leaders must use AI as an enabler, not a substitute. A message generated by AI should always be reviewed, contextualized, and delivered in a leader's authentic voice.

The danger of overreliance is clear: when employees or customers sense communication is entirely machine-driven, credibility suffers. The most effective leaders use AI to scale communication without sacrificing humanity.

Case Study: AI in Customer Service at Scale

Airlines and banks have been among the most aggressive adopters of AI chatbots for customer service. One global airline implemented an AI-powered support system that reduced call center demand by 40%. Importantly, the system was designed to hand off seamlessly to human agents for complex cases. Customer satisfaction rose not because AI replaced humans, but because it freed humans to focus where empathy was most needed.

The Takeaway

AI is transforming communication by making it faster, more personalized, and more scalable. Chatbots, assistants, and personalization engines extend leaders' ability to connect without being overwhelmed. But growth in the AI era depends on balance: using AI to scale communication while ensuring messages remain authentic, human, and aligned with organizational values.

Using AI for Strategic Forecasting and Market Analysis

In a world defined by rapid change, leaders cannot rely solely on intuition or static reports to guide strategy. They need foresight—an ability to see where markets are heading before competitors do. Artificial intelligence is revolutionizing forecasting and market analysis, giving leaders a dynamic edge in navigating uncertainty and seizing opportunity.

From Historical Data to Predictive Insight

Traditional forecasting relies heavily on historical data and linear projections. While useful, this approach struggles in volatile environments where past trends no longer predict the future. AI changes the equation by analyzing vast, diverse datasets—from economic indicators to social media sentiment—to uncover patterns invisible to humans.

For example:

- **Retail**: AI predicts demand for products by analyzing weather forecasts, local events, and consumer search behavior.
- **Finance**: Algorithms monitor real-time market signals, geopolitical events, and even news sentiment to anticipate fluctuations.
- **Healthcare**: Predictive models forecast disease outbreaks by tracking travel patterns, climate data, and online health searches.

AI doesn't just extend traditional forecasting—it transforms it from reactive to anticipatory.

Market Analysis at Scale

Leaders once relied on consultants or small research teams to study competitors and markets. Today, AI-powered tools continuously scan millions of data points across industries. They:

- Track competitor pricing, product launches, and hiring trends.
- Analyze customer reviews and social conversations for unmet needs.
- Identify emerging startups and disruptive technologies.

This real-time intelligence allows leaders to act before opportunities become obvious—or before risks become crises.

Scenario Planning with AI

Beyond predicting likely outcomes, AI enhances **scenario planning** by modeling multiple futures. Leaders can test "what if" situations:

- What if raw material costs spike 20%?
- What if a competitor launches an AI-driven product next quarter?
- What if regulation shifts in a key market?

By simulating these possibilities, leaders can design strategies that are resilient under different conditions.

Benefits for Leaders

1. **Faster Decisions** – Real-time forecasting allows leaders to respond before markets shift.
2. **Smarter Resource Allocation** – Investment decisions are guided by predictive demand signals.
3. **Competitive Advantage** – Market moves can be anticipated rather than followed.
4. **Resilience** – Scenario planning prepares organizations for shocks, from supply chain disruptions to geopolitical shifts.

Case Study: AI in Retail Forecasting

Walmart uses AI to predict demand across its massive inventory, integrating data from weather, social trends, and purchasing behavior. During hurricanes, AI systems anticipate surges not only in emergency supplies but also in unexpected items like strawberry Pop-Tarts—a phenomenon identified by analyzing past storm data. This precision allows Walmart to stock shelves proactively, meeting customer needs while competitors react.

The Leadership Imperative

AI is a powerful forecasting ally, but it is not infallible. Leaders must:

- Validate AI insights with human judgment.
- Ensure transparency in models to avoid black-box decisions.
- Use AI as a guide, not a dictator.

The Takeaway

AI-powered forecasting and market analysis give leaders the ability to see around corners. They transform uncertainty into opportunity by surfacing insights that guide faster, smarter, and more resilient strategies. Growth in the AI era will belong to leaders who combine predictive intelligence with vision and judgment, steering their organizations with confidence in a turbulent world.

CHAPTER 6

Leading Digital Transformation Projects

Creating a Digital-First Vision for Your Organization

Digital transformation begins not with technology, but with vision. Leaders who succeed in the AI era understand that adopting new tools is not enough—organizations must reimagine themselves as digital-first. This means weaving data, AI, and technology into the fabric of strategy, culture, and operations. Without a clear vision, digital initiatives risk becoming fragmented projects rather than drivers of transformation.

Why Vision Matters

A digital-first vision provides direction in an environment of constant change. It answers questions such as:

- What role will digital play in delivering value to our customers?
- How will AI reshape our core business model?
- How do we want our organization to operate five years from now?

Without this vision, AI adoption often becomes reactive: a tool added here, an experiment run there, but no unifying purpose. With vision, every initiative aligns with a broader transformation strategy.

Characteristics of a Digital-First Vision

1. **Customer-Centric** – Technology is not the goal; better customer experiences are. Leaders must articulate how digital tools will create deeper personalization, faster service, and stronger relationships.
2. **Data-Driven** – A digital-first vision positions data as a strategic asset, not a byproduct. It emphasizes building the infrastructure and culture needed to make decisions from real-time insights.

3. **AI-Enabled** – AI is not an optional add-on; it is a core enabler of innovation, efficiency, and foresight.
4. **Inclusive and Human-Centered** – Digital transformation must empower employees, not alienate them. A vision that ignores the workforce creates resistance rather than momentum.

Case Study: Starbucks' Digital Vision

Starbucks offers a clear example of digital-first leadership. Its leaders envisioned the mobile app not just as a convenience tool but as the centerpiece of the customer experience. By integrating AI-driven personalization into the app, Starbucks created one of the most successful loyalty programs in the world, with over half of U.S. sales now coming through digital channels. The vision was not simply "use AI"—it was to transform customer engagement.

Communicating the Vision

A digital-first vision only drives change if it is communicated clearly and consistently. Leaders must:

- Share the vision in plain language, avoiding technical jargon.
- Connect the vision to employee values and career growth.
- Reiterate it regularly, showing how each project contributes to the larger goal.

When employees see the link between AI adoption and the organization's purpose, they are more likely to embrace transformation rather than resist it.

Avoiding Common Pitfalls

- **Technology-Centric Vision**: A vision framed solely around tools ("we will adopt AI everywhere") risks alienating employees and confusing stakeholders. Vision must always tie back to human value.

- **Short-Term Thinking**: Digital-first is not a one-year initiative; it is an ongoing evolution. Leaders must set long-term goals while celebrating short-term wins.
- **Exclusion of Workforce**: Failing to involve employees in shaping the vision creates fear and resistance.

The Takeaway

Creating a digital-first vision is the foundation of leading transformation. It defines not just how technology will be used, but why it matters for customers, employees, and society. Growth in the AI era depends on leaders who can see beyond tools to the possibilities they unlock, guiding their organizations with clarity, confidence, and purpose.

Aligning AI Adoption with Business Goals

AI adoption delivers the greatest value when it is tied directly to business goals. Too often, organizations fall into the trap of adopting AI for its own sake—launching pilots or experimenting with tools without a clear link to strategy. This leads to wasted resources, disjointed efforts, and disillusionment among employees. Leaders must ensure that AI is not a side project but a core enabler of the organization's mission.

Why Alignment Matters

AI is not just another IT upgrade—it is a strategic capability. When aligned with business goals, it accelerates growth, improves customer experiences, and strengthens competitiveness. When misaligned, it creates noise and drains resources.

For example, a retailer whose goal is to deepen customer loyalty should focus on AI tools that personalize recommendations and enhance service—not on adopting AI in areas that do not affect customer engagement. The clarity of alignment determines whether AI creates measurable impact or fades into obscurity.

Steps to Align AI with Strategy

1. **Start with Business Priorities** – Identify the top organizational goals: revenue growth, customer retention, operational efficiency, market expansion. Then ask: *Where can AI have the biggest impact?*
2. **Define Success Metrics** – Establish how AI initiatives will be measured. Is the goal reduced churn, faster supply chains, or increased sales per customer? Clear metrics keep projects focused.
3. **Pilot with Purpose** – Small experiments are valuable, but they must connect to larger business goals. A pilot that cannot scale to support strategy is just a distraction.
4. **Integrate, Don't Isolate** – AI should not sit in a separate innovation lab disconnected from the business. It must be embedded into core functions where impact is highest.

Case Study: Delta Airlines

Delta aligned AI adoption with its core goal: improving customer experience. By deploying AI for predictive maintenance, the airline reduced flight delays—a direct driver of customer satisfaction and loyalty. Instead of adopting AI broadly without focus, Delta applied it strategically where it mattered most, turning technology into competitive advantage.

Avoiding the "Shiny Object" Trap

Leaders often face pressure to chase the latest AI trend—chatbots, generative AI, or predictive models—without asking how it connects to the organization's strategy. The result is fragmented projects that fail to deliver value.

The test for leaders is simple: **If an AI initiative does not support a business goal, why pursue it?** By asking this question, leaders avoid the trap of chasing hype and instead focus on meaningful transformation.

Aligning Culture with Goals

Alignment is not only technical—it is cultural. Employees must understand how AI connects to the organization's mission. Leaders should:

- Communicate how AI supports shared goals.
- Involve teams in shaping initiatives.
- Celebrate wins that show AI delivering business value.

When employees see the connection, adoption accelerates.

The Takeaway

AI adoption without alignment is wasted effort. Leaders must ensure every initiative ties back to business goals, with clear metrics and cultural buy-in. Growth in the AI era will not come from adopting AI everywhere, but from adopting it where it matters most—where it amplifies strategy, delivers value, and strengthens competitive advantage.

Frameworks for Scaling AI Solutions (Pilot → Adoption → Integration)

Many organizations experiment with AI pilots, but few succeed in scaling them into enterprise-wide impact. The difference lies not in technology but in leadership. Without a clear framework for scaling, AI remains a set of isolated experiments. With one, it becomes a driver of transformation. Leaders must understand the stages of AI adoption—pilot, adoption, and integration—and how to navigate each effectively.

Stage 1: Pilot – Testing Possibilities

Pilots are valuable for testing feasibility and learning quickly. At this stage, organizations experiment with limited AI applications in controlled environments.

- **Purpose**: Validate the technology, uncover potential value, and test cultural readiness.
- **Example**: A bank pilots an AI chatbot for one product line to assess how customers respond.

Leadership at this stage should focus on learning, not perfection. The goal is to identify opportunities, challenges, and potential ROI before scaling.

Stage 2: Adoption – Expanding Use Cases

Once pilots prove value, the next stage is adoption—rolling out AI across more functions and geographies.

- **Purpose**: Move from isolated use cases to broader application.
- **Example**: After a successful chatbot pilot, the bank expands it across all customer service channels.

At this stage, leaders must address scalability challenges: data integration, governance, employee training, and change management. Adoption succeeds when leaders balance speed with structure.

Stage 3: Integration – Embedding AI into the Core

Integration is where AI moves from being a project to becoming part of the organization's DNA. It is no longer an add-on; it underpins strategy, culture, and daily operations.

- **Purpose**: Ensure AI is embedded across the value chain.
- **Example**: The bank integrates AI not only into customer service but also into fraud detection, compliance, risk management, and product design.

At this stage, leadership must ensure ethical standards, transparency, and continuous learning. Integration is not the end of a project—it is the beginning of a new way of working.

The Scaling Framework

To move effectively from pilot to integration, leaders should follow a structured framework:

1. **Define Business Alignment** – Ensure pilots support strategic goals, not just technical curiosity.
2. **Measure ROI Early** – Establish metrics that demonstrate value, even at small scale.
3. **Invest in Infrastructure** – Build data pipelines, cloud capacity, and governance frameworks for scalability.
4. **Prepare the Workforce** – Train employees for new roles and workflows.
5. **Institutionalize Learning** – Capture insights from pilots to refine broader strategy.

Case Study: Global Retailer

A global retailer piloted AI for inventory forecasting in one region. After proving accuracy gains, it adopted the system across multiple regions. Eventually, AI was integrated into every aspect of operations—from supply chain logistics to personalized marketing. What began as a pilot became a global transformation, saving billions in costs and driving growth.

The Takeaway

Scaling AI requires moving deliberately through pilot, adoption, and integration. Leaders must provide structure, alignment, and cultural readiness at every stage. Growth in the AI era will not come from scattered pilots but from integrated systems that reshape how organizations think, operate, and deliver value.

Budgeting and ROI for AI Projects

AI promises extraordinary value, but realizing that value requires thoughtful investment. Unlike traditional IT upgrades, AI projects often begin as experiments, scale unpredictably, and deliver returns in both tangible and intangible forms. Leaders must therefore rethink how they approach budgeting and ROI. The goal is not just to fund technology but to maximize impact while managing risk.

Why Budgeting for AI Is Different

Traditional budgeting assumes predictability: upfront costs, clear timelines, and defined outputs. AI projects are more fluid. They evolve as algorithms learn, data improves, and use cases expand. This creates uncertainty in both cost and return.

For example, training a generative AI model may require ongoing cloud expenses, specialized talent, and data acquisition. The payoff may not come immediately as revenue, but as improved efficiency, better customer engagement, or competitive differentiation.

Principles for AI Budgeting

1. **Start Small, Scale Smart** – Begin with focused pilots that test feasibility before committing large budgets.
2. **Balance CapEx and OpEx** – Many AI costs are operational (cloud usage, subscriptions, data labeling). Leaders must shift mindset from one-time investment to continuous funding.
3. **Invest in Talent and Training** – Tools alone are insufficient; budget must include reskilling employees and attracting AI-savvy talent.
4. **Plan for Infrastructure** – Robust data pipelines, governance, and security systems are critical hidden costs.

Measuring ROI Beyond Dollars

ROI for AI projects must be measured broadly. Financial returns matter, but leaders must also capture strategic and cultural value.

- **Efficiency Gains**: Reduced costs through automation (e.g., faster claims processing in insurance).
- **Revenue Growth**: New products, services, or markets enabled by AI.
- **Customer Experience**: Improved personalization, reduced churn, stronger loyalty.
- **Risk Reduction**: Better fraud detection, compliance monitoring, or predictive maintenance.
- **Employee Engagement**: Time freed from repetitive work, greater job satisfaction, higher retention.

By tracking multiple dimensions, leaders build a more accurate picture of AI's value.

Case Study: AI in Logistics

A global shipping company invested in AI-driven route optimization. Initial ROI was modest—fuel savings of 5%. However, as the system scaled, benefits multiplied: fewer late deliveries, happier customers, reduced carbon footprint, and lower insurance costs due to fewer accidents. Over time, the compounded ROI far exceeded initial projections. Leaders who accounted only for short-term savings would have underestimated its impact.

Avoiding Pitfalls

- **Chasing Vanity Projects**: Some leaders fund AI because it looks innovative rather than because it aligns with strategy.
- **Underestimating Ongoing Costs**: AI systems require continuous tuning, monitoring, and governance.
- **Overemphasizing Short-Term ROI**: Focusing only on immediate payback risks missing transformational opportunities.

The Leadership Role

Leaders must balance ambition with discipline:

- Set clear expectations that AI is a long-term investment.
- Demand measurable outcomes while remaining open to non-financial value.
- Communicate to boards and stakeholders that ROI will compound over time.

The Takeaway

Budgeting and ROI for AI projects require a new mindset. Leaders must embrace continuous investment, measure impact beyond financial metrics, and recognize that returns often grow exponentially as systems scale. Growth in the AI era belongs to those who budget boldly but wisely—funding not just technology, but the infrastructure, talent, and trust that make AI transformative.

Case Studies: Successful vs. Failed Digital Transformation Initiatives

Not all digital transformation journeys are equal. Some organizations harness AI and digital technologies to reinvent themselves, achieving industry leadership. Others stumble, wasting millions on projects that never scale or deliver value. Studying these contrasts helps leaders understand what separates success from failure.

Success Story: Microsoft's Cloud and AI Reinvention

When Satya Nadella became CEO in 2014, Microsoft faced stagnation. Rather than chasing short-term wins, Nadella pursued a bold digital-first vision centered on cloud computing and AI. The company integrated AI into core products like Office 365, Azure, and Teams, while making responsible AI a strategic pillar.

Why it worked:

- Clear vision aligned with business goals.
- Focus on customer value rather than technology for its own sake.
- Scaled AI across functions, not as isolated pilots.
- Invested in talent and culture to support transformation.

The result: Microsoft became one of the most valuable companies in the world, reshaping enterprise technology through AI.

Success Story: DBS Bank's Digital-First Culture

DBS, a Singapore-based bank, transformed itself from a traditional financial institution into one of the world's most digital-first banks.

It embraced AI for fraud detection, customer personalization, and predictive services. Crucially, it cultivated a culture where employees were encouraged to think and act like a startup.

Why it worked:

- Strong leadership commitment to digital-first vision.
- Integration of AI into customer and employee experiences.
- Cultural transformation alongside technological adoption.

DBS went from being seen as "difficult to deal with" to being recognized as the world's best bank multiple years in a row.

Failure Story: Sears' Digital Hesitation

Sears had opportunities to adopt AI-driven e-commerce strategies early, yet leadership failed to prioritize digital transformation. While competitors like Amazon and Walmart used AI for supply chain optimization, personalization, and logistics, Sears relied on outdated systems and resisted change.

Why it failed:

- Lack of alignment between digital initiatives and business goals.
- Cultural resistance to change.
- Underinvestment in technology and talent.

The result: Sears filed for bankruptcy, a cautionary tale of what happens when leaders fail to act decisively in the digital era.

Failure Story: Quibi's Misaligned Vision

Quibi, the short-form video streaming startup, raised nearly $2 billion to disrupt media. Despite heavy investment in technology, it collapsed within months of launch.

Why it failed:

- Vision not aligned with customer demand.
- Technology was novel but not integrated with a clear value proposition.
- Leadership underestimated competitors already leveraging AI to personalize and distribute content.

Quibi proves that money and technology alone cannot guarantee success—alignment and execution are everything.

Lessons from Success and Failure

From these case studies, the patterns are clear:

- **Vision matters**: Leaders must articulate a digital-first vision tied to customer value.
- **Culture is critical**: Transformation fails without cultural buy-in and adaptability.
- **Integration beats isolation**: AI must be embedded across the business, not siloed.
- **Speed counts**: Hesitation allows competitors to seize advantage.

The Takeaway

Successful digital transformations are not about adopting the latest technology—they are about visionary leadership, cultural readiness, and strategic alignment. Failures come from hesitation, misalignment, or treating AI as a side project. Growth in the AI era will belong to leaders who combine bold vision with disciplined execution, ensuring that technology amplifies strategy rather than distracts from it.

CHAPTER 7

Ethics, Trust, and Responsible Leadership

AI Bias, Transparency, and Accountability in Decision-Making

Artificial intelligence is only as good as the data and assumptions that shape it. When leaders deploy AI without addressing bias, transparency, and accountability, they risk undermining trust and causing harm. In the AI era, responsible leadership requires not only asking what AI *can* do, but also whether it is doing so fairly and openly.

Understanding AI Bias

Bias in AI occurs when algorithms produce systematically unfair outcomes, often reflecting imbalances in the data used to train them. If historical hiring data favors certain demographics, an AI recruiting tool may replicate and even amplify those biases.

Examples include:

- Facial recognition systems that misidentify people of color at higher rates.
- Loan approval algorithms that disadvantage applicants from certain neighborhoods.
- Predictive policing tools that reinforce existing patterns of over-surveillance.

Bias is not always intentional, but its impact is real. Leaders must recognize that bias in AI is not a technical flaw alone—it is an ethical and leadership failure if left unaddressed.

The Role of Transparency

Traditional decision-making often relied on leaders' credibility. In the AI era, opaque algorithms—so-called "black boxes"—challenge that credibility. If employees, customers, or regulators cannot understand how decisions are made, trust erodes.

Transparency means ensuring AI systems are explainable: stakeholders should be able to know why a decision was made. For example, if an AI denies a customer a loan, leaders must provide clear, human-readable reasons—not hide behind "the algorithm decided."

Transparency is not only ethical; it is strategic. It fosters trust, reduces resistance, and strengthens credibility.

Accountability in the AI Era

AI may make recommendations, but accountability always lies with leaders. Delegating decisions to algorithms does not absolve leadership of responsibility. If an AI system causes harm, the question is not *what went wrong with the algorithm* but *what went wrong with leadership oversight*.

Accountability requires:

- Establishing governance frameworks to monitor AI decisions.
- Regularly auditing systems for bias and unintended consequences.
- Creating escalation processes where humans intervene in high-stakes decisions.

Case Study: Amazon's Biased Recruiting Tool

Amazon once tested an AI recruiting tool trained on historical hiring data. Because past hiring favored men, the system began downgrading resumes that included indicators of being female (e.g., participation in women's clubs). Amazon ultimately scrapped the project. The failure was not in experimenting with AI, but in insufficient oversight of bias and accountability. Leaders learned that without ethical guardrails, AI can magnify inequities.

The Leadership Imperative

Leaders cannot treat AI ethics as a side issue for compliance teams. Bias, transparency, and accountability are central to trust and brand reputation. Customers will not accept opaque systems that discriminate. Employees will not embrace tools they perceive as unfair. Regulators will not hesitate to act against irresponsible use.

Responsible leaders:

- Set ethical standards before deploying AI.
- Demand explainability and fairness in every system.
- Accept ultimate responsibility for AI-driven decisions.

The Takeaway

AI bias, transparency, and accountability are not technical issues—they are leadership issues. Leaders must ensure that AI systems are fair, explainable, and overseen with responsibility. Growth in the AI era will depend not only on innovation but also on trust. The organizations that win will be those whose leaders prove that intelligence—human or artificial—serves fairness, integrity, and accountability.

Data Privacy and Security as a Leadership Responsibility

In the digital era, data is one of the most valuable assets an organization holds. It fuels AI systems, enables personalization, and drives strategic insights. But with this power comes profound responsibility. Mishandling data—whether through weak security, careless use, or lack of transparency—can erode trust overnight. Leaders must treat data privacy and security not as technical concerns for IT teams alone, but as core leadership responsibilities.

Why Privacy and Security Matter

Every AI system relies on data, often personal and sensitive: customer transactions, employee performance, medical histories, or financial details. A breach or misuse does not just create operational disruption—it damages credibility and trust.

Examples abound:

- Equifax's 2017 data breach exposed sensitive financial information of 147 million people, leading to reputational collapse and billions in penalties.
- Healthcare organizations that mishandle patient data face not only fines but also loss of trust in life-or-death contexts.

In the AI era, leaders cannot afford to see data as an abstract resource. Every dataset represents people whose trust must be earned and protected.

The Leader's Role in Data Stewardship

1. **Setting the Tone** – Leaders must communicate that privacy and security are organizational priorities, not compliance checkboxes.
2. **Embedding Governance** – Strong policies for data collection, storage, and usage should be part of corporate governance.
3. **Investing in Protection** – Budgeting for cybersecurity infrastructure is as essential as investing in AI itself.
4. **Empowering Teams** – Employees at all levels should be trained to handle data responsibly, recognizing that one weak link can compromise the system.

Balancing Innovation with Responsibility

A common tension in AI adoption is between using data to innovate and protecting privacy. Leaders must navigate this balance carefully:

- Overly restrictive policies can stifle innovation.
- Lax policies create risk of misuse and breaches.

The solution lies in **privacy by design**—building systems that minimize data exposure, anonymize where possible, and give individuals control over their information. Leaders who prioritize responsible innovation send a powerful message: progress does not come at the cost of trust.

Case Study: Apple's Privacy-First Strategy

Apple has made privacy a cornerstone of its brand. By introducing features such as on-device processing and giving users control over app tracking, Apple positioned itself as a trusted guardian of data. This leadership choice not only differentiated the company but also reinforced customer loyalty. Leaders in other industries can learn from this approach: data protection is not just a legal requirement but a competitive advantage.

Preparing for Inevitable Breaches

Even the strongest systems can be attacked. Responsible leaders prepare by:

- Establishing clear incident response plans.
- Communicating transparently with stakeholders if breaches occur.
- Taking accountability rather than shifting blame.

Trust is not lost when mistakes happen—it is lost when leaders fail to respond with integrity.

The Takeaway

Data privacy and security are not IT problems—they are leadership imperatives. Protecting data means protecting people, trust, and reputation. Leaders in the AI era must ensure that innovation is matched with responsibility. Growth will belong to organizations whose leaders prove that data can be used powerfully and ethically, without compromising the trust of those they serve.

Building Trust with Employees, Customers, and Stakeholders

In the AI era, trust is not a byproduct of good leadership—it is the foundation. As organizations adopt AI to automate decisions, analyze personal data, and reshape business models, stakeholders demand confidence that these systems are fair, transparent, and aligned with human values. Leaders who fail to build trust face resistance, reputational risk, and regulatory scrutiny. Leaders who succeed gain loyalty, resilience, and long-term advantage.

Trust with Employees

Employees are often the first to feel the impact of AI adoption. They worry about job security, fairness in AI-driven evaluations, and the role of technology in their daily work. Leaders must:

- **Communicate openly**: Explain how AI is being used, what it means for roles, and how employees will be supported.
- **Empower through training**: Provide opportunities for upskilling and reskilling so employees see AI as a growth opportunity rather than a threat.
- **Involve employees in design**: Encourage teams to provide feedback during AI implementation, fostering ownership rather than resistance.

When employees trust leaders to use AI responsibly, adoption accelerates, and morale strengthens.

Trust with Customers

Customers are increasingly aware that their data fuels AI. They expect personalization, speed, and accuracy—but not at the expense of privacy or fairness. Leaders must ensure:

- **Transparency**: Customers know what data is collected and how it is used.
- **Control**: Customers can set preferences and opt out where desired.
- **Fairness**: AI-driven systems avoid bias that could harm or exclude certain groups.

For example, fintech companies that clearly explain credit scoring algorithms build stronger customer relationships than those that hide behind opaque systems.

Trust with Stakeholders and Society

AI adoption also raises broader societal concerns: Will automation worsen inequality? Will algorithms discriminate? Will organizations prioritize profit over responsibility? Leaders must engage with these questions openly.

- **Investors** increasingly evaluate companies on ESG (environmental, social, governance) performance, including AI ethics.
- **Regulators** demand compliance with data privacy, transparency, and fairness standards.
- **Communities** expect organizations to use AI in ways that benefit society, not exploit vulnerabilities.

By proactively addressing these concerns, leaders strengthen credibility and avoid crises that erode public trust.

Case Study: DBS Bank

DBS Bank in Singapore earned trust by being transparent in how it used AI for customer personalization. It communicated openly with customers, ensured strong data protections, and emphasized fairness. This trust not only improved adoption of digital services but also positioned DBS as one of the world's most respected financial institutions.

The Role of Consistency

Trust is built through consistent behavior. Leaders cannot claim to prioritize fairness while deploying opaque AI systems that disadvantage stakeholders. Each decision signals values. Consistency between words and actions is what transforms promises into trust.

The Takeaway

Building trust in the AI era is not optional—it is a leadership mandate. Employees, customers, and stakeholders must see that AI is deployed with fairness, transparency, and responsibility. Growth will belong to leaders who understand that in a world where technology changes quickly, trust remains the most enduring competitive advantage.

Global Regulations and Compliance Leaders Must Know

AI is advancing faster than most legal frameworks, but regulations are rapidly emerging worldwide. For leaders, compliance is not just a legal obligation—it is a test of responsibility and foresight. Understanding and anticipating global regulations ensures organizations avoid costly penalties, maintain trust, and position themselves as ethical leaders in the digital era.

Why Leaders Must Care

AI systems touch sensitive domains: personal data, employment, healthcare, finance, and public safety. Governments recognize the risks of bias, misuse, and surveillance, and they are responding with regulation. Leaders who dismiss these shifts expose their organizations to legal, financial, and reputational risks.

Key Global Frameworks

1. **European Union: The AI Act**
   The EU is leading with one of the most comprehensive AI regulatory frameworks. The AI Act classifies systems by risk levels—from minimal risk (chatbots) to high risk (biometric surveillance, healthcare, finance). High-risk systems face strict requirements for transparency, human oversight, and accountability.

Leadership implication: Any global company operating in Europe must design AI systems with compliance in mind from the start.

2. **United States: Sector-Based Regulation**
   The U.S. does not yet have a single AI law but enforces regulations across sectors—such as healthcare (HIPAA), finance (SEC guidelines), and employment (EEOC standards). Additionally, the White House has issued the **AI Bill of Rights**, emphasizing principles of fairness, transparency, and accountability.

Leadership implication: U.S. leaders must monitor evolving federal and state-level laws, especially in high-stakes sectors.

3. **China: Algorithm and Deep Synthesis Regulations**
   China has introduced rules on recommendation algorithms and deep synthesis (deepfakes), requiring platforms to prevent misuse and label synthetic content. The government emphasizes both control and innovation, making compliance complex but essential.

Leadership implication: Companies in China must balance rapid innovation with strict oversight and censorship rules.

4. **Other Jurisdictions**

- **Canada**: Developing the Artificial Intelligence and Data Act (AIDA), focusing on responsible innovation.
- **Singapore**: Promoting voluntary frameworks such as the Model AI Governance Framework.
- **Global Organizations**: OECD and UNESCO have issued ethical AI guidelines that influence policymaking.

Challenges for Leaders

- **Fragmentation**: Regulations vary by region, requiring global organizations to adapt strategies for each market.
- **Evolving Standards**: Laws are new and evolving, creating uncertainty for long-term planning.
- **Balancing Innovation and Compliance**: Overly cautious compliance may stifle innovation, while neglect invites penalties.

Building Compliance into Leadership

Leaders must:

- **Embed compliance in design**: Build "ethics and compliance by design" into AI development.
- **Invest in monitoring**: Regularly audit AI systems for adherence to local and international standards.
- **Stay proactive**: Anticipate future regulations by aligning with global best practices, not just minimum legal requirements.

Case Study: Multinational Financial Institution

A global bank operating across Europe, the U.S., and Asia created an AI governance board to monitor regulatory developments. By harmonizing compliance processes and adopting EU-level standards globally, it not only reduced legal risk but also built customer trust. Competitors that treated compliance reactively faced higher costs and reputational setbacks.

The Takeaway

Global AI regulation is no longer theoretical—it is here. Leaders who ignore compliance put their organizations at risk. Those who embrace it proactively build resilience, trust, and competitive advantage. Growth in the AI era will belong to leaders who treat regulation not as a barrier, but as a framework for responsible innovation.

Ethical Frameworks for Sustainable AI Leadership

As AI becomes embedded in business and society, leaders face a defining question: not just *can* we build this, but *should* we? Sustainable AI leadership requires ethical frameworks that guide innovation, balance stakeholder interests, and ensure long-term trust. Without them, organizations risk short-term gains at the cost of lasting credibility.

Why Ethical Frameworks Matter

AI systems shape decisions in healthcare, hiring, finance, and beyond. Without ethical guardrails, they can reinforce inequality, exploit privacy, or prioritize profit over human well-being. Ethical frameworks help leaders:

- Ensure fairness and inclusivity.
- Protect privacy and autonomy.
- Maintain accountability and transparency.
- Align innovation with human values.

These are not abstract ideals—they are competitive advantages in a market where customers, employees, and regulators demand responsibility.

Core Principles of Ethical AI Leadership

1. **Fairness** – AI systems must avoid bias and discrimination. This requires diverse datasets, continuous auditing, and oversight.
2. **Transparency** – Decisions made by AI must be explainable in human terms. Black-box models erode trust.
3. **Accountability** – Leaders remain responsible for outcomes, even when algorithms make recommendations.

4. **Privacy and Security** – Data should be handled with the highest standards of protection and consent.
5. **Sustainability** – AI initiatives should consider long-term social and environmental impact, not just short-term gain.

Applying Ethical Frameworks in Practice

Ethical frameworks are effective only when operationalized:

- **Governance Structures**: Establish ethics committees or AI oversight boards to review projects.
- **Guidelines and Training**: Educate employees on responsible AI use, from engineers to business leaders.
- **Impact Assessments**: Evaluate potential harm before deploying systems, especially in high-stakes areas.
- **Feedback Loops**: Allow customers and employees to raise concerns and ensure they are addressed transparently.

Case Study: Google's AI Principles

After public backlash over controversial AI projects, Google established a set of AI principles emphasizing fairness, accountability, and social benefit. While implementation has been uneven, the framework provided a foundation for decision-making and signaled commitment to ethical leadership. The lesson for leaders: ethical frameworks must be more than statements—they require consistent action.

The Role of Global Standards

Leaders can also draw on international frameworks to guide practice:

- **OECD AI Principles** – Promote human-centered values and fairness.
- **UNESCO AI Ethics Recommendation** – Highlights inclusivity and sustainability.

- **ISO Standards for AI** – Provide practical guidelines for responsible implementation.

By aligning with global norms, leaders future-proof their organizations against evolving regulation and societal expectations.

Ethical Leadership as Competitive Advantage

Ethical AI leadership is not a constraint—it is an enabler. Companies known for fairness and transparency attract top talent, win customer loyalty, and avoid costly scandals. In a world where reputation spreads instantly, ethical consistency is one of the most valuable assets leaders can cultivate.

The Takeaway

Sustainable AI leadership rests on ethical frameworks that balance innovation with responsibility. Fairness, transparency, accountability, privacy, and sustainability must guide every AI decision. Growth in the AI era will not come only from technological breakthroughs, but from leaders who prove that intelligence—human and artificial—serves society as much as shareholders.

CHAPTER 8

Your Roadmap to Becoming an AI Leader

Assessing Your Current Leadership Style in the AI Context

Becoming an AI leader does not begin with adopting tools—it begins with self-awareness. Leaders must first understand how their current style aligns with the demands of the AI era. This assessment provides the foundation for growth, helping leaders identify strengths to leverage and gaps to close.

Why Self-Assessment Matters

The AI era introduces new challenges: leading human–AI collaboration, making data-driven decisions, and managing ethical complexity. Leaders who cling to outdated approaches risk losing relevance. By assessing their style honestly, leaders can adapt before disruption forces the change.

Self-assessment is not about judgment—it is about clarity. It helps leaders ask: *Am I prepared to lead in a world where intelligence is shared between humans and machines?*

Key Dimensions of Leadership in the AI Era

1. **Decision-Making Style**
   o Traditional: Relies heavily on intuition and experience.
   o AI-Enhanced: Balances intuition with data-driven insights, using AI as a decision partner.
   o Self-check: Do I welcome AI insights, or do I see them as a challenge to my authority?
2. **Approach to Innovation**
   o Traditional: Waits for proven models before acting.
   o AI-Ready: Experiments early, learns quickly, and scales responsibly.
   o Self-check: Do I encourage pilots and experimentation, or do I avoid risk?

3. **Ethical Orientation**
    - o Traditional: Focuses on compliance as a minimum standard.
    - o AI-Ready: Proactively addresses bias, fairness, and transparency.
    - o Self-check: Do I see ethics as a checkbox or as a strategic advantage?
4. **People Leadership**
    - o Traditional: Directs teams through hierarchy and control.
    - o AI-Ready: Empowers teams, fosters collaboration with AI, and invests in reskilling.
    - o Self-check: Do my employees see AI as a threat or as an opportunity under my leadership?

Tools for Self-Assessment

- **360-Degree Feedback**: Collect input from peers, direct reports, and mentors on how you handle technology-driven change.
- **Leadership Style Surveys**: Use instruments that measure adaptability, openness to data, and comfort with ambiguity.
- **AI Literacy Tests**: Gauge your understanding of AI concepts, opportunities, and risks.
- **Personal Reflection**: Keep a leadership journal, asking regularly: *How did I use data today? How did I balance efficiency with ethics?*

Case Example: Transitioning Leadership Style

A manufacturing CEO known for decisive, intuition-driven leadership realized his style was mismatched for AI adoption. After conducting a self-assessment, he acknowledged resistance to data-driven insights. By committing to change, he began involving data scientists in strategic discussions and showcasing his own learning journey. Over time, his shift inspired cultural change across the company.

Turning Awareness into Action

Assessment is valuable only if it leads to growth. Once leaders identify their style, they must:

- Double down on strengths that align with AI leadership.
- Create development plans to address weaknesses.
- Surround themselves with advisors and teams who complement their blind spots.

The Takeaway

Assessing your leadership style is the first step to becoming an AI leader. It requires honesty, openness, and humility. Growth in the AI era will come not from knowing everything, but from recognizing where you stand today and committing to the journey of evolution.

Setting Your AI Leadership Vision and Goals

Once leaders assess their current style, the next step is to define where they want to go. An AI leadership journey cannot be left to chance—it requires a clear vision and concrete goals. Vision provides direction, while goals translate that vision into actionable steps. Together, they form the roadmap for growth in the AI era.

Why Vision Matters in AI Leadership

AI is not simply a set of tools; it is a force that reshapes industries, jobs, and decision-making. Without vision, leaders risk being reactive—adopting AI piecemeal in response to competitors or crises. With vision, leaders position AI as a driver of innovation and long-term advantage.

Vision answers questions like:

- How will AI redefine our industry in five to ten years?
- What role do I want my organization to play in that future?
- How will I ensure AI serves not only shareholders but also employees, customers, and society?

Translating Vision into Goals

A vision without goals remains abstract. Goals anchor ambition to measurable progress. In the AI leadership context, effective goals should be:

- **Specific** – Targeted toward particular outcomes (e.g., implement AI-powered customer service within 12 months).
- **Measurable** – Tied to KPIs like customer satisfaction, efficiency gains, or revenue impact.
- **Achievable** – Ambitious but realistic, considering current capabilities.
- **Relevant** – Directly aligned with organizational priorities.
- **Time-Bound** – Framed within clear timelines to create accountability.

Examples of AI Leadership Goals

- **Personal Development Goal**: "Within six months, I will complete an AI leadership certification and begin applying insights to my team's strategy."
- **Organizational Goal**: "By next year, we will implement AI-driven forecasting in our supply chain to reduce costs by 10%."
- **Cultural Goal**: "We will launch a company-wide AI literacy program to ensure every employee understands how AI supports our mission."

Balancing Ambition and Responsibility

Effective AI goals go beyond performance—they embed ethics and responsibility. For example, a leader's vision may be to become the most data-driven organization in the industry. The corresponding goal must also ensure fairness, privacy, and transparency in AI use. Growth without responsibility risks reputational and regulatory backlash.

Case Example: Vision and Goals at a Global Bank

A global bank set a vision to become "the most trusted AI-driven financial institution." Its leadership established three concrete goals:

1. Implement AI fraud detection across all markets within two years.
2. Ensure every AI system undergoes bias testing before deployment.
3. Train 80% of employees in AI literacy within three years.

This alignment of vision and goals positioned the bank not only as an innovator but also as a responsible leader.

The Takeaway

Setting a vision and defining goals are essential steps in becoming an AI leader. Vision gives direction; goals create accountability. Leaders who combine ambition with responsibility ensure their organizations not only adopt AI but do so with purpose, ethics, and measurable impact.

The 90-Day Plan: Small Steps to Start Leading with AI Today

Big visions and long-term goals are essential, but they can feel distant without immediate action. The 90-day plan bridges this gap, giving leaders a structured way to begin leading with AI right now. By breaking the journey into small, practical steps, leaders build momentum, demonstrate progress, and signal commitment to their teams.

Why 90 Days?

Ninety days is long enough to make meaningful progress but short enough to sustain focus. It creates urgency without overwhelming scope. A clear 90-day plan also reassures employees and stakeholders that AI leadership is not just talk—it is action.

Step 1: Build Personal AI Literacy (Weeks 1–3)

Leaders cannot delegate understanding of AI entirely to experts. The first step is to develop personal fluency:

- Learn the basics of AI capabilities and limitations.
- Experiment with AI tools such as chatbots, generative AI platforms, or decision dashboards.
- Attend a workshop, webinar, or certification program focused on AI for leaders.

This is not about becoming a data scientist—it is about speaking the language of AI and leading with confidence.

Step 2: Identify a High-Impact Pilot (Weeks 4–6)

Choose one pilot project aligned with business goals. The criteria should be:

- Clear connection to strategy (e.g., improving customer experience or operational efficiency).
- Manageable scope for 90 days.
- Measurable outcomes to demonstrate impact.

Example: A retail leader might pilot an AI tool for personalized marketing campaigns to increase engagement.

Step 3: Engage and Educate the Team (Weeks 7–9)

AI leadership is not a solo act—it requires team buy-in. During this phase:

- Communicate openly about the pilot's purpose and expected benefits.
- Offer training so employees feel confident using AI tools.
- Encourage feedback and address concerns transparently.

The goal is to build trust and show that AI is here to empower, not replace, people.

Step 4: Measure and Share Results (Weeks 10–12)

At the end of the 90 days, leaders must evaluate outcomes and share results:

- What worked well, and what challenges emerged?
- How did the pilot support business goals?
- What lessons can be scaled to other parts of the organization?

Sharing results builds credibility and creates momentum for broader adoption.

Case Example: 90-Day Pilot in Logistics

A logistics company leader launched a 90-day pilot using AI for route optimization in one region. Within three months, delivery times improved by 12% and fuel costs dropped by 8%. The leader showcased these results to employees and executives, creating enthusiasm for expanding AI adoption across the supply chain.

Building Momentum Beyond 90 Days

The 90-day plan is not the end—it is the beginning of a cycle. Each quarter, leaders can:

- Launch new pilots in different functions.
- Expand successful initiatives.
- Deepen AI literacy across the organization.

The Takeaway

The 90-day plan turns aspiration into action. By focusing on literacy, piloting, engagement, and measurement, leaders create immediate wins and lay the foundation for long-term transformation. Growth in the AI era belongs to leaders who start small but act decisively, proving that AI leadership is not about the distant future—it starts today.

The Long-Term Roadmap: Becoming a Visionary Leader in the Digital Era

While a 90-day plan establishes momentum, true AI leadership requires a long-term roadmap. Visionary leaders understand that AI is not a passing trend but a general-purpose technology that will shape entire industries for decades. The challenge is not only to adopt AI but to evolve continuously alongside it.

Thinking in Horizons

Effective long-term planning unfolds across three horizons:

1. **Horizon 1 – Strengthen the Present**
   Embed AI in existing processes to improve efficiency, reduce costs, and deliver immediate value. Examples: predictive maintenance in manufacturing or AI-driven personalization in retail.
2. **Horizon 2 – Expand the Possible**
   Use AI to develop new products, services, and business models. Examples: healthcare providers offering AI-driven preventive care or banks creating AI-based financial coaching platforms.
3. **Horizon 3 – Redefine the Future**
   Anticipate disruptive changes where AI reshapes entire industries. Examples: autonomous enterprises or industries built around AI-generated content.

Visionary leaders keep all three horizons in play, balancing short-term wins with long-term transformation.

Building Organizational Capabilities

A long-term roadmap requires leaders to invest in capabilities that endure beyond individual projects:

- **Talent Pipelines**: Develop continuous upskilling programs and partnerships with universities to attract AI-ready talent.
- **Data Infrastructure**: Build robust systems that ensure scalability, security, and ethical use of data.
- **Ethical Governance**: Establish enduring frameworks for fairness, accountability, and transparency.
- **Innovation Culture**: Foster a mindset where experimentation is celebrated and failure is seen as learning.

Milestones on the Roadmap

- **Year 1–2**: Widespread AI literacy across the organization, with pilots scaled into multiple functions.
- **Year 3–5**: AI integrated into core business strategy, creating measurable improvements in revenue, customer experience, and efficiency.
- **Year 5–10**: New AI-driven business models emerge, positioning the organization as an industry leader.
- **Beyond 10 Years**: Organization evolves into an adaptive, AI-empowered enterprise with global influence.

Case Example: Visionary Leadership in Retail

Walmart's long-term AI roadmap shows how incremental and transformative goals coexist. It began with Horizon 1 efficiencies— demand forecasting and logistics optimization. It expanded into Horizon 2 by developing AI-powered e-commerce personalization. Today, it is exploring Horizon 3 with autonomous delivery systems. This layered roadmap ensures continuous relevance and leadership.

The Leadership Role

Becoming a visionary AI leader requires:

- **Patience**: Recognizing that transformation unfolds over years, not quarters.
- **Courage**: Investing boldly in AI even before the path is fully clear.
- **Adaptability**: Revisiting and adjusting the roadmap as technology and society evolve.
- **Responsibility**: Ensuring growth aligns with ethics, trust, and societal good.

The Takeaway

The long-term roadmap transforms leaders from adopters to visionaries. By thinking across horizons, building enduring capabilities, and committing to ethics and adaptability, leaders ensure their organizations are not just AI-ready but AI-resilient. Growth in the digital era will belong to those who see AI not as a project to finish, but as a journey to lead—shaping industries, societies, and the future itself.

Future-Proofing Your Career and Organization in the Age of Intelligent Machines

AI is not a passing disruption—it is a permanent transformation of how work, leadership, and industries operate. Leaders who want to thrive must think beyond short-term adoption and focus on future-proofing both their own careers and their organizations. This requires adaptability, foresight, and a commitment to continuous evolution.

Future-Proofing Your Career

Leaders must recognize that their personal leadership style, skills, and knowledge must evolve alongside technology. To remain relevant:

- **Embrace Lifelong Learning**: Commit to continuous education in AI, data literacy, and digital leadership. Stay curious, attending workshops, certifications, and industry conferences.
- **Develop Tech Fluency**: You don't need to code, but you must understand AI's capabilities, risks, and applications well enough to make informed strategic decisions.
- **Strengthen Human Skills**: AI excels at analysis and automation, but leadership still requires empathy, ethical judgment, and vision. These are irreplaceably human and will only grow in value.
- **Build Adaptive Networks**: Surround yourself with advisors, peers, and cross-industry connections who can provide fresh perspectives on how AI is changing work.

Future-proofing your career means becoming the type of leader who grows as fast as technology evolves.

Future-Proofing Your Organization

Organizations that survive disruption are those designed for adaptability. Leaders can future-proof by:

1. **Embedding Continuous Learning**: Establish upskilling and reskilling programs so employees can evolve with technology.
2. **Investing in Scalable Infrastructure**: Build flexible data systems and cloud platforms that support rapid adoption of emerging AI tools.
3. **Creating Agile Structures**: Replace rigid hierarchies with agile teams that can pivot quickly in response to change.

4. **Focusing on Ethics and Trust**: Prioritize transparency, fairness, and privacy to build resilience against regulatory and reputational risks.
5. **Exploring Emerging Trends**: Stay ahead by experimenting with frontier AI developments such as autonomous agents, multimodal AI, or AI-human collaboration platforms.

Case Example: Future-Proofing in Automotive

Tesla demonstrates organizational future-proofing by treating its cars not just as vehicles but as platforms. By building cars with updatable AI-driven software, Tesla ensures each product improves over time, adapting to new technologies and consumer demands. The lesson: organizations that design for evolution stay relevant long after their competitors stagnate.

The Leader's Mindset for the Future

Future-proofing is less about predicting the future than about preparing for multiple futures. Leaders must:

- Accept uncertainty as a constant.
- Build resilience into systems, culture, and strategy.
- Approach AI not as a one-time project, but as an ongoing journey.

The Takeaway

Future-proofing your career and organization is about adaptability, learning, and responsibility. Leaders who continuously grow their own skills, design organizations for agility, and prioritize ethics will not only survive disruption but shape it. Growth in the age of intelligent machines belongs to those who prepare for change—not by fearing it, but by embracing it as the foundation of leadership in the digital era.

Glossary

AI (Artificial Intelligence) – The simulation of human intelligence in machines that can perform tasks such as learning, reasoning, and problem-solving.

AI Agent – An autonomous system that can perform multi-step tasks across applications, adapt to changing inputs, and make decisions without constant human oversight.

Bias in AI – Systematic errors in AI outputs caused by imbalanced or flawed training data, leading to unfair or discriminatory outcomes.

Data Governance – The policies, processes, and standards that ensure data is accurate, secure, and used responsibly.

Decision Support System (DSS) – An AI-powered platform that analyzes data, simulates scenarios, and provides recommendations to aid decision-making.

Digital-First Vision – A leadership approach that prioritizes digital technologies, AI, and data as central to strategy, culture, and operations.

Ethical AI – The practice of designing and using AI in ways that are fair, transparent, accountable, and aligned with human values.

Explainability – The ability of an AI system to provide clear, understandable reasoning for its outputs or decisions.

Generative AI – AI that creates new content—text, images, audio, or video—based on patterns learned from data.

Machine Learning (ML) – A subset of AI where algorithms improve performance over time by learning from data.

Predictive Analytics – The use of AI and statistical techniques to analyze current and historical data to make predictions about future events.

Reskilling – Training employees for entirely new roles created by technological change.

Transparency – The principle that AI decisions should be explainable and understandable to stakeholders.

Upskilling – Teaching employees new skills to enhance their performance in their current roles.

A Personal Note from the Author

Thank you for joining me on this journey through *Lead with AI*. Writing this book has been about more than exploring technology—it has been about exploring leadership in a time of profound change. My hope is that the insights, strategies, and case studies you've read will help you not just navigate the AI era but thrive as a leader within it.

If this book has given you clarity, inspiration, or actionable ideas, I would be truly grateful if you could take a few minutes to leave a review on Amazon. Your feedback helps other readers discover the book and join this movement toward responsible, visionary AI leadership.

Your voice matters, and your support means the world. Together, we can shape a future where technology amplifies the best of human leadership.

— *Eric LeBouthillier*

www.ingramcontent.com/pod-product-compliance
Lightning Source LLC
Chambersburg PA
CBHW071710210326
41597CB00017B/2417